Jazz Gems
FOR SOLO GUITAR

T0053189

ISBN 978-0-634-06667-2

Visit Hal Leonard Online at
www.halleonard.com

World headquarters, contact:
Hal Leonard
7777 West Bluemound Road
Milwaukee, WI 53213
Email: info@halleonard.com

In Europe, contact:
Hal Leonard Europe Limited
42 Wigmore Street
Marylebone, London, W1U 2RY
Email: info@halleonardeurope.com

In Australia, contact:
Hal Leonard Australia Pty. Ltd.
4 Lentara Court
Cheltenham, Victoria, 3192 Australia
Email: info@halleonard.com.au

PREFACE

This book contains 35 professional chord melody arrangements for solo guitar. The selections come from some of the finest composers of the 20th century, and are well known by musicians and singers. The book is for guitarists who want to learn chord melody arrangements, new chords, when and how to use them, and when and how to put bass lines within chords. You'll also learn that just because a chord has a long name, it doesn't have to be difficult to play!

This is my fourth solo guitar chord melody arrangement book for the Hal Leonard Corporation. It differs from the previous books due to the use of even more sophisticated and unusual chords. For example, note the unique chord voicings found in the standards "I Should Care" and "East of the Sun."

Melody, lyrics, and rhythm give a certain feel to a song, but chords have their own personalities that can greatly affect the mood as well. Through my choice of chords I have tried to enhance the feel of a song. For instance, I have tried to make pretty songs beautiful by using major seventh chords. Conversely, for sad songs, I have used dramatic, brooding chords.

It is my desire that the study of this book, as well as my others, will make your solo guitar playing more fruitful and enjoyable. Think of each chord as a word, and then put those words together to tell your own arrangement story. Your ears will get bigger and so will your pride!

—Robert B. Yelin

DEDICATION

This book is dedicated to Ken Roughton, Alan Donaldson, Wayne Atebara, Kate Connors, Dick Atkins, Michael Coppola, Richard McGowen, Ben Neiman, Gus DeGazio, Lennie Stelos, Ray Martorelli, Steve Mesple, Gil Parris, Monroe Quinn, Bill Kuhlman, Jeff Arnold, Jeff Schroedl, and all other guitarists who strive to be the best that they can be. A big thanks to the Hal Leonard crew, and a loving hug to Johnny Smith. My whole heart thanks my exceptional friend and wife, Harriet, who has lived with all my ups and downs and, "Oh my gosh! You bought another guitar!" For twenty five years she has done everything to make me well, happy, and strong. Without her, I could never have written my books. Without her, there would be no music. I'm so fortunate to share our strong love.

CONTENTS

After You've Gone

Words by Henry Creamer
Music by Turner Layton

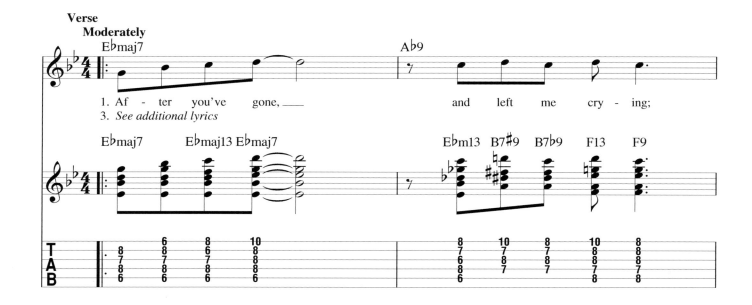

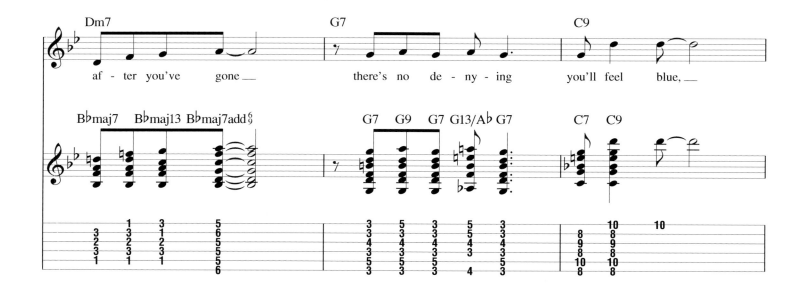

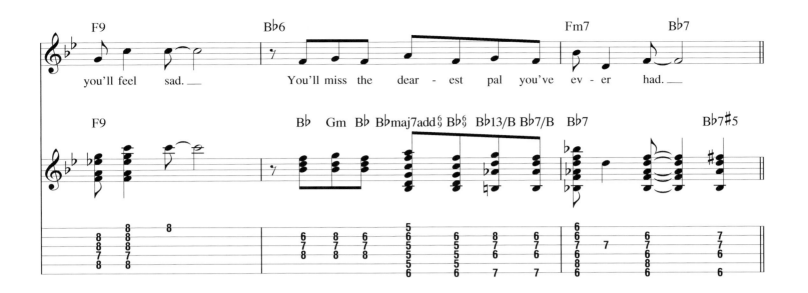

you'll feel sad. — You'll miss the dear - est pal you've ev - er had. —

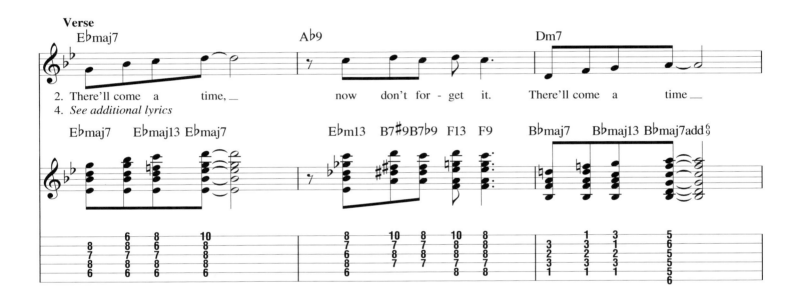

Verse

2. There'll come a time, — now don't for - get it. There'll come a time —
4. *See additional lyrics*

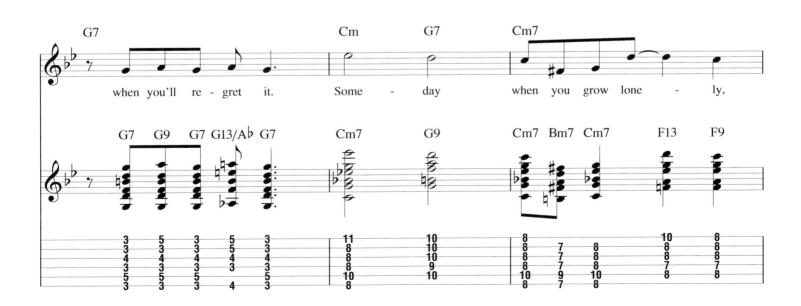

when you'll re - gret it. Some - day when you grow lone - ly,

Additional Lyrics

3. After I'm gone, after we break up;
   After I'm gone, you're gonna wake up.
   You will find you were blind
   To let somebody come and change your mind.

4. After the years we've been together,
   Their joys and tears, all kinds of weather.
   Someday blue and down-hearted,
   You'll long to be with me right back where you started.
   After I'm gone, after I'm gone away.

Alfie

Theme from the Paramount Picture ALFIE

Words by Hal David
Music by Burt Bacharach

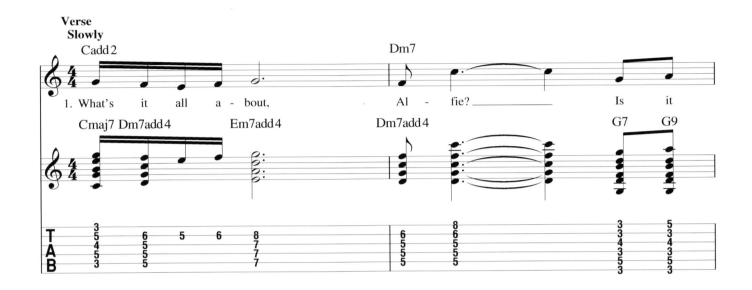

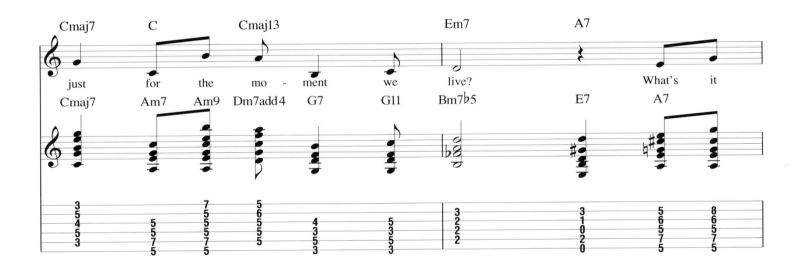

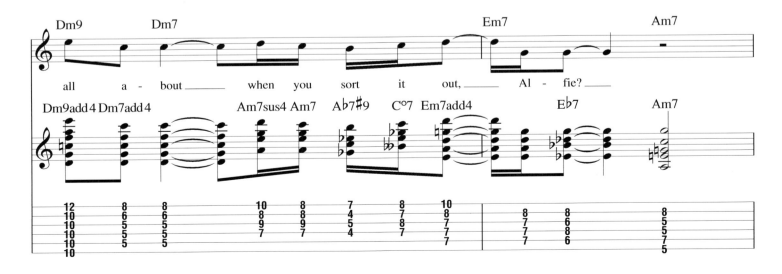

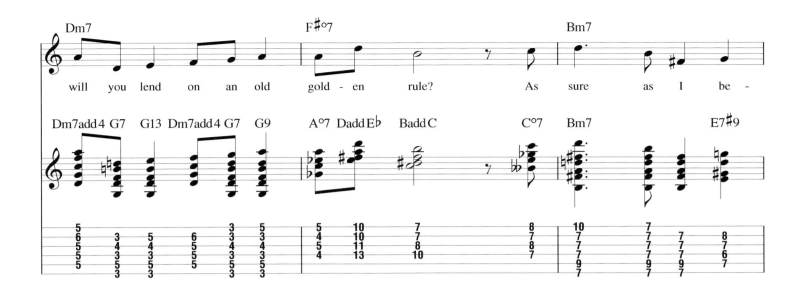

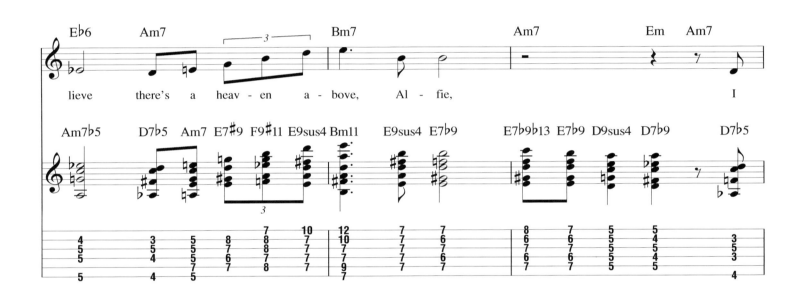

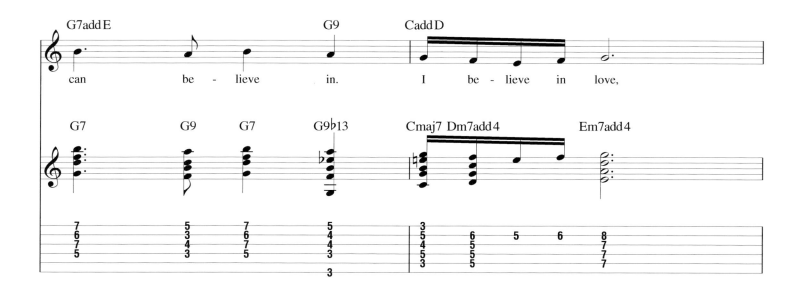

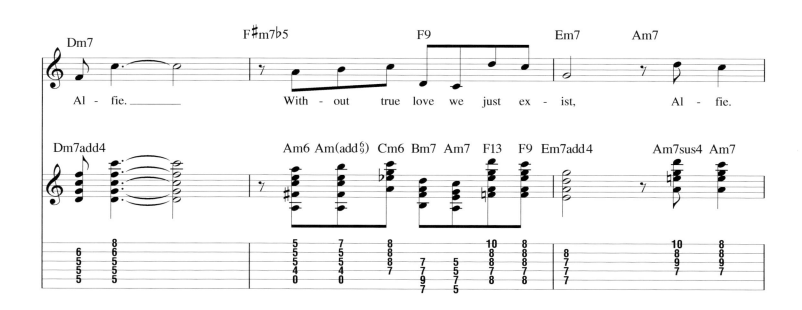

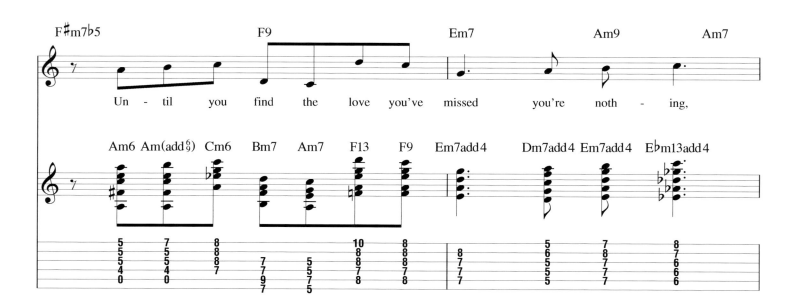

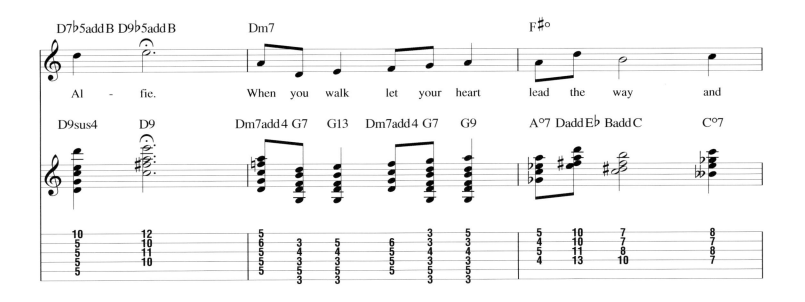

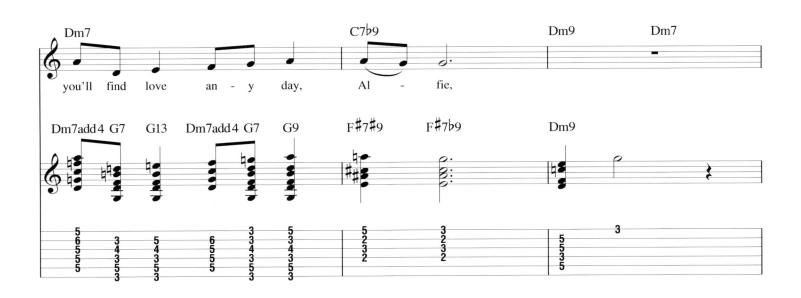

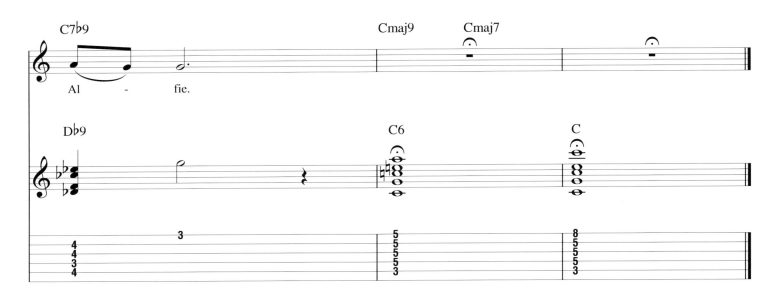

Alice in Wonderland

from Walt Disney's ALICE IN WONDERLAND

Words by Bob Hilliard
Music by Sammy Fain

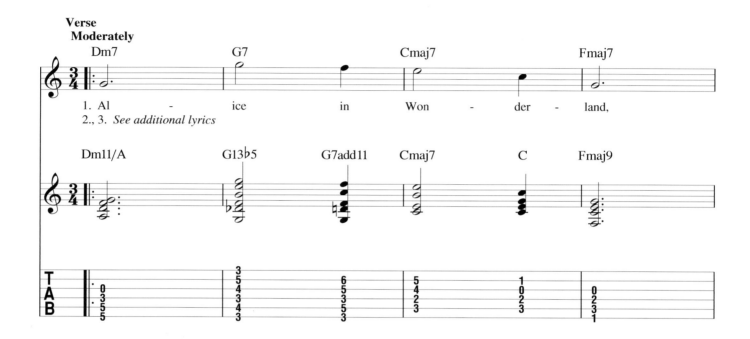

1. Al - ice in Won - der - land,
2., 3. *See additional lyrics*

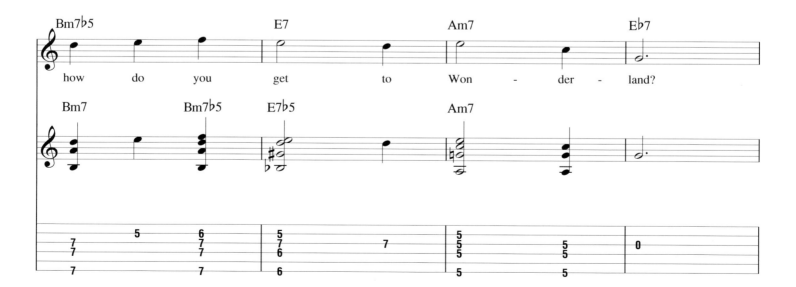

how do you get to Won - der - land?

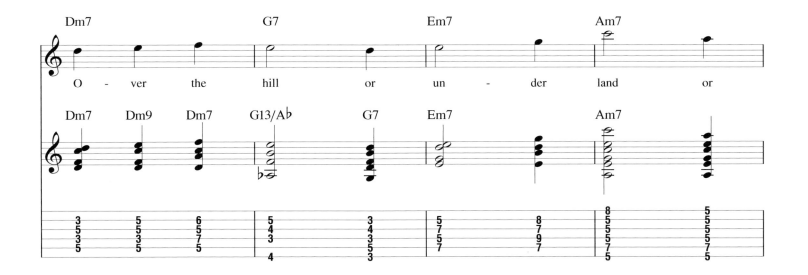

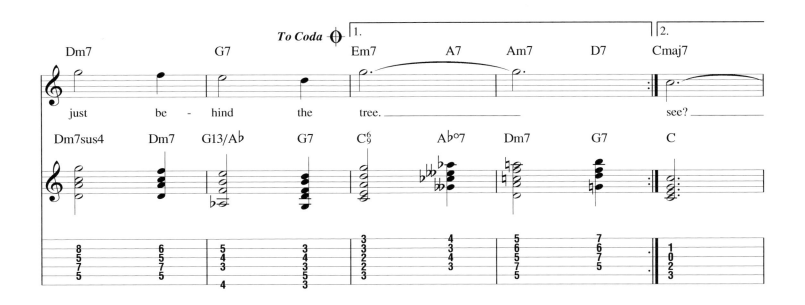

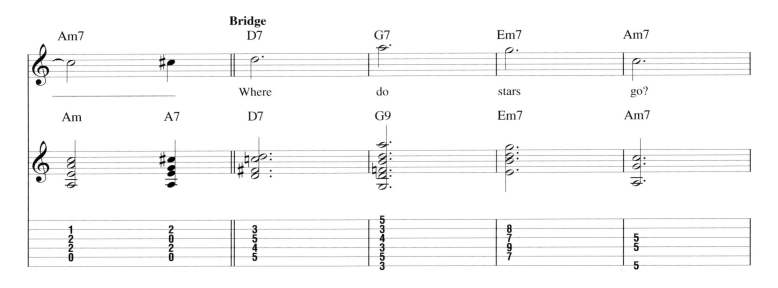

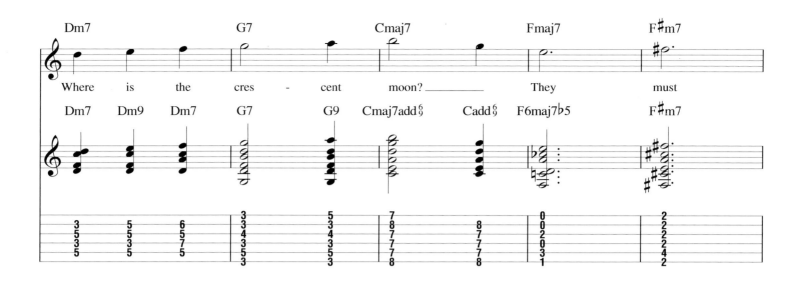

Where is the cres - cent moon? _____ They must

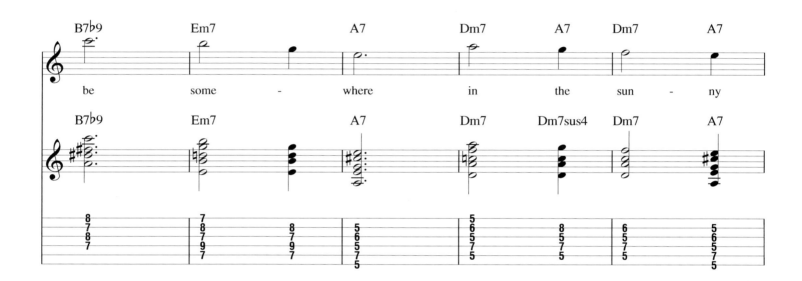

be some - where in the sun - ny

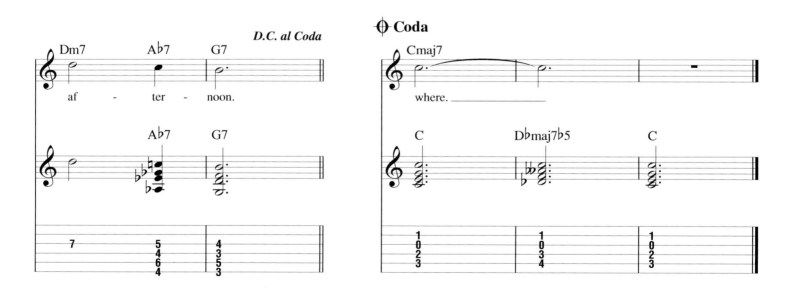

D.C. al Coda

af - ter - noon.

Coda

where. _____

Additional Lyrics

2. Alice in Wonderland,
   How do you get to Wonderland?
   Over the hill or under land
   Or just behind the tree.

3. Alice in Wonderland,
   Where is the path to Wonderland?
   Over the hill or here or there?
   I wonder where.

Do Nothin' Till You Hear From Me

Words and Music by Duke Ellington and Bob Russell

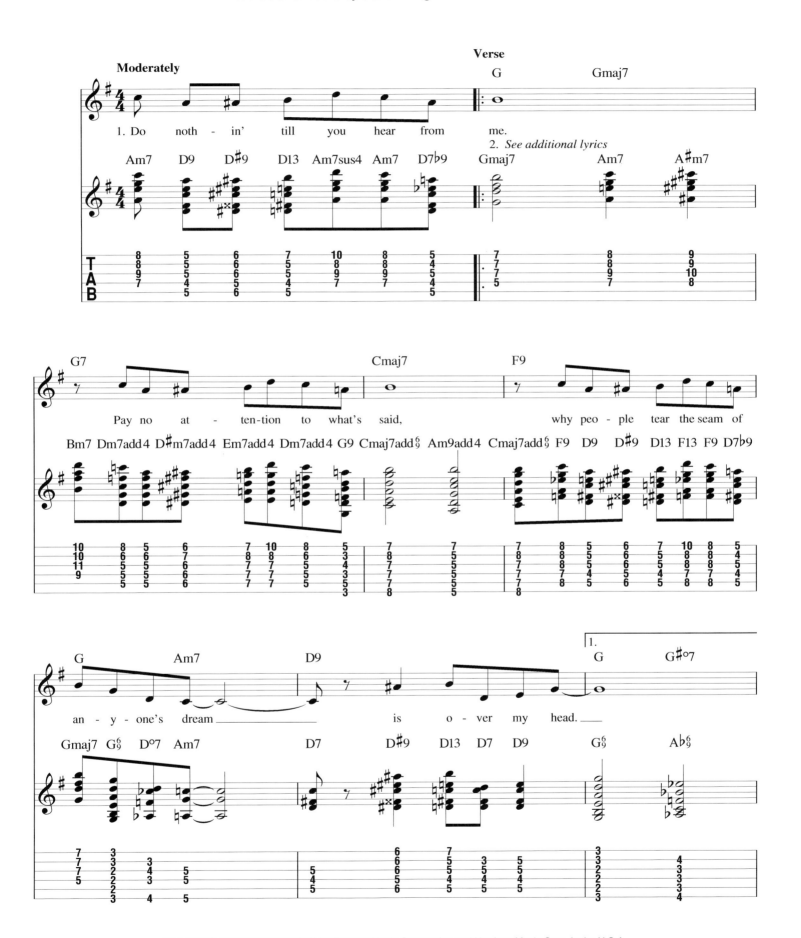

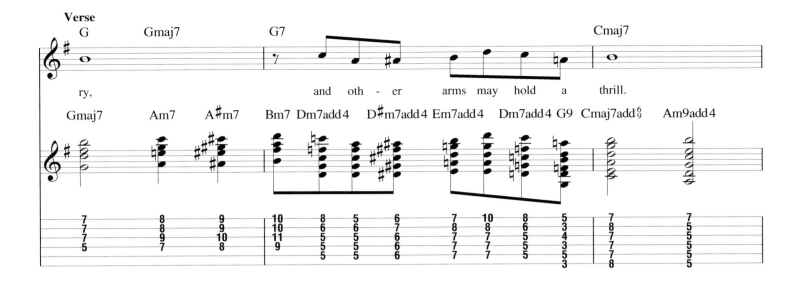

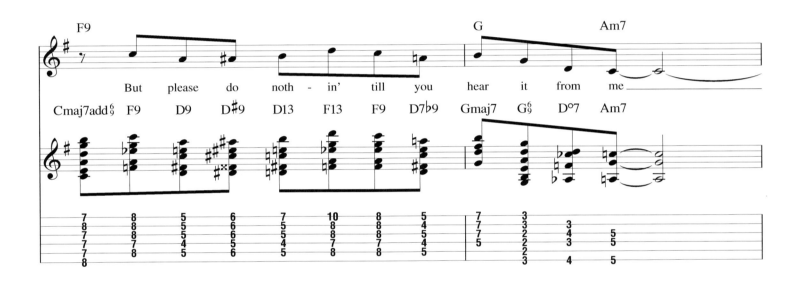

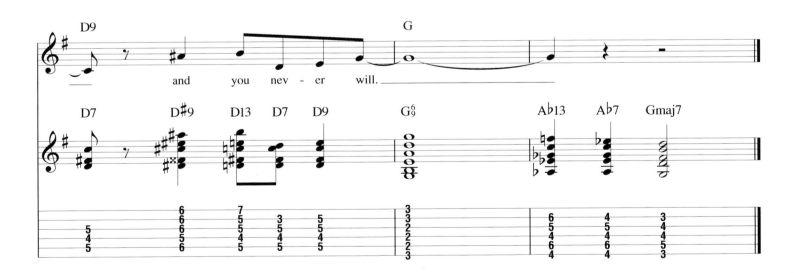

Additional Lyrics

2. Do nothin' till you hear from me,
At least consider our romance.
If you should take the word of others you've heard
I haven't a chance.

Along Came Betty

By Benny Golson

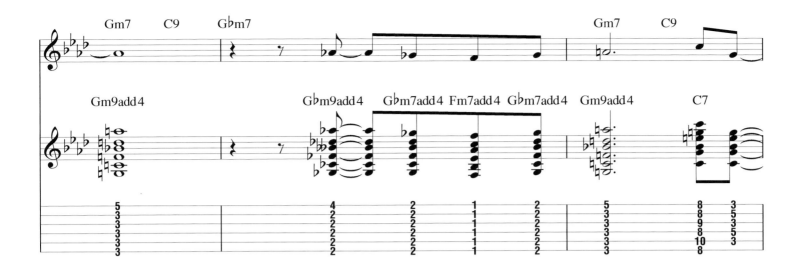

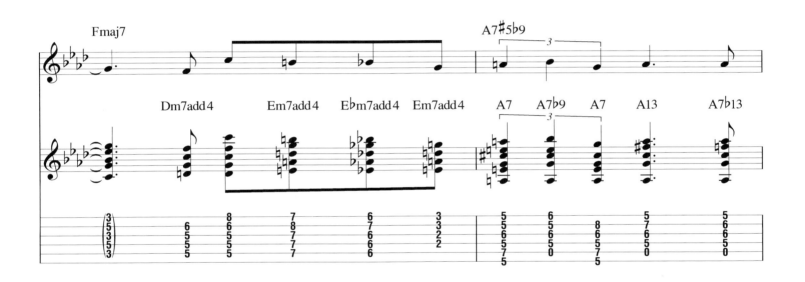

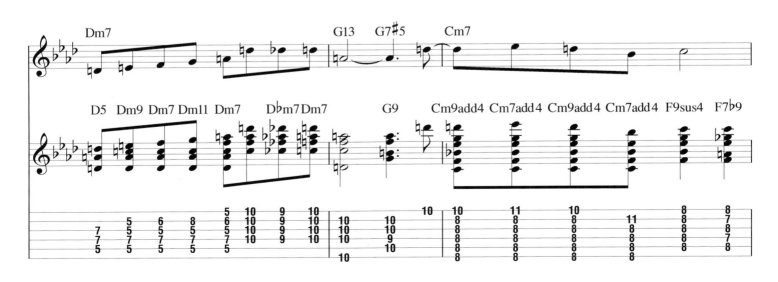

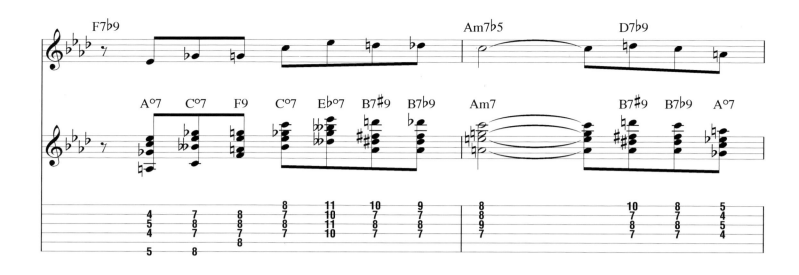

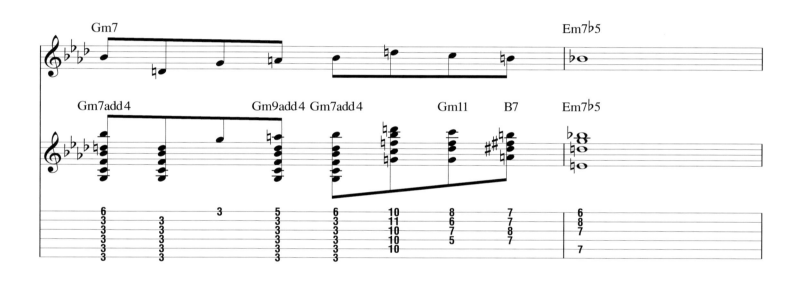

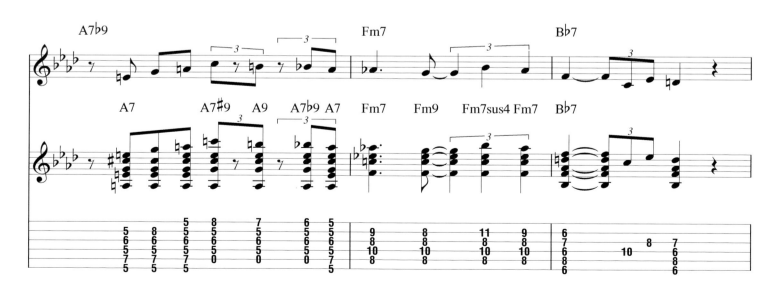

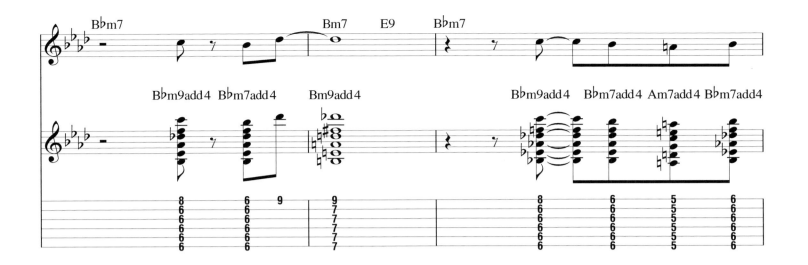

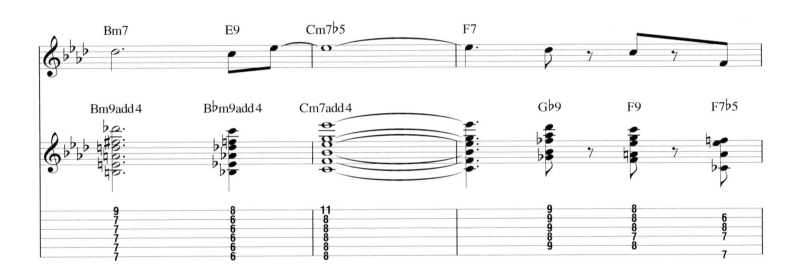

The Breeze and I

Words by Al Stillman
Music by Ernesto Lecuona

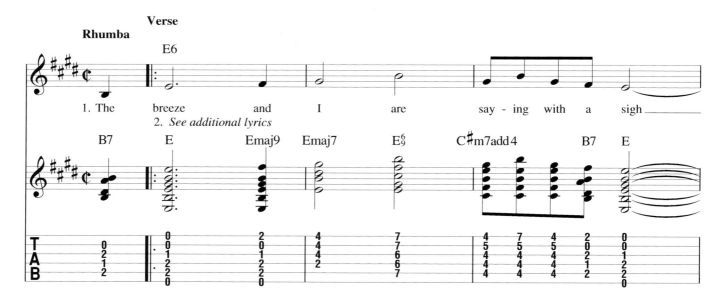

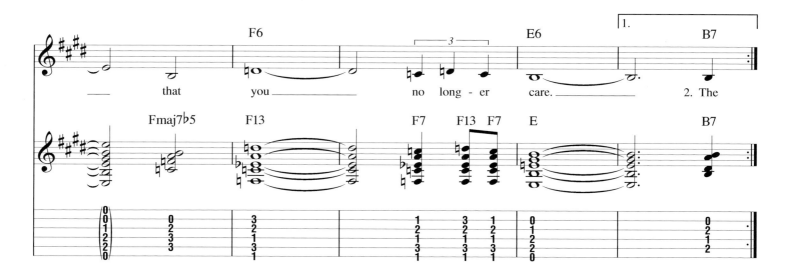

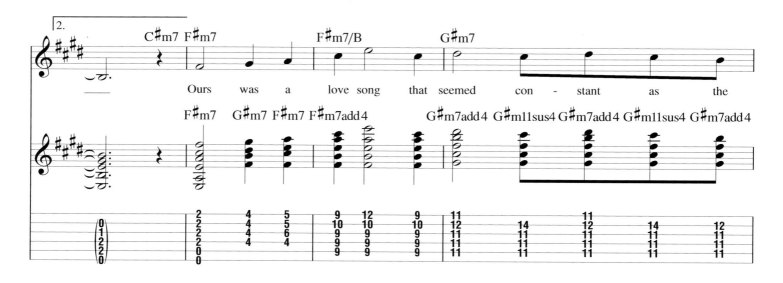

Additional Lyrics

2. The breeze and I are whispering goodbye
   To dreams we used to share.

Chelsea Bridge

By Billy Strayhorn

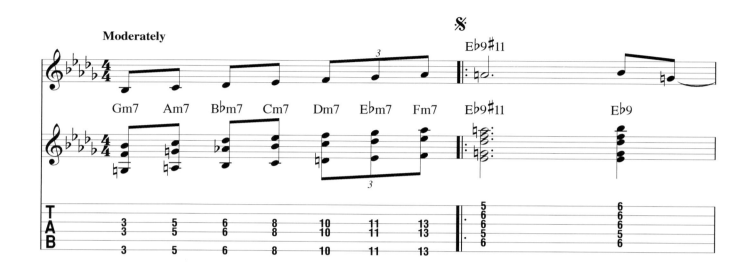

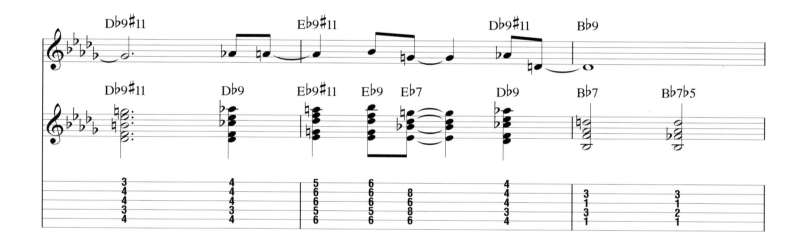

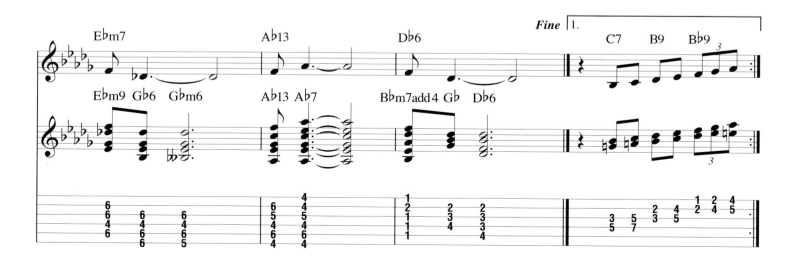

A Child Is Born

Music by Thad Jones
Lyrics by Alec Wilder

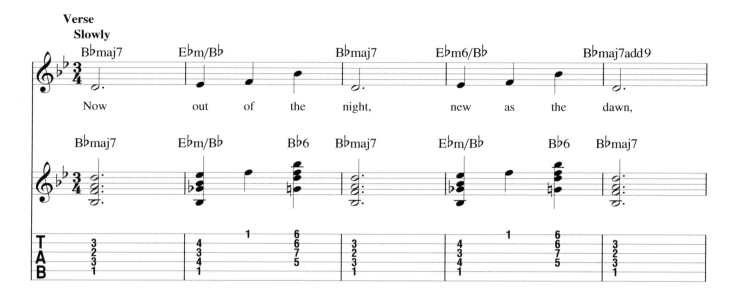

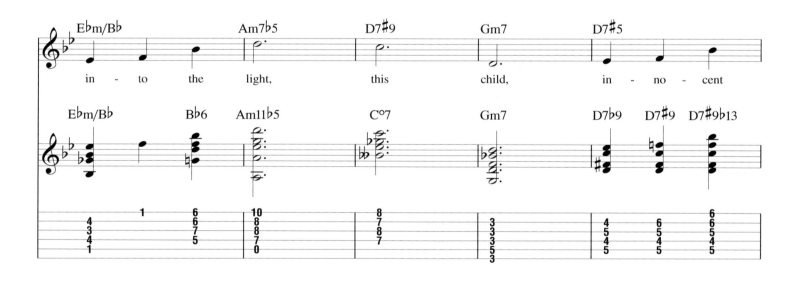

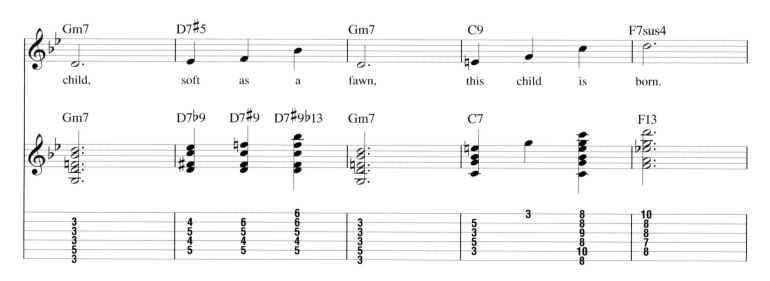

The Christmas Song
(Chestnuts Roasting on an Open Fire)

Music and Lyric by Mel Torme and Robert Wells

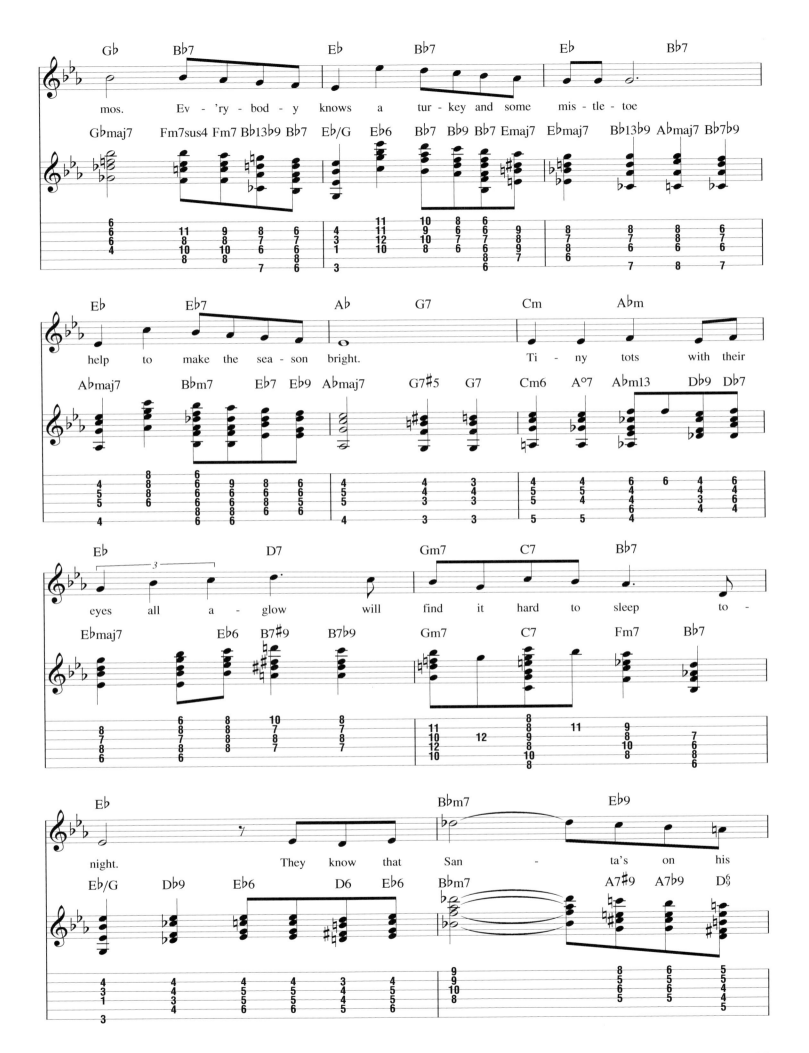

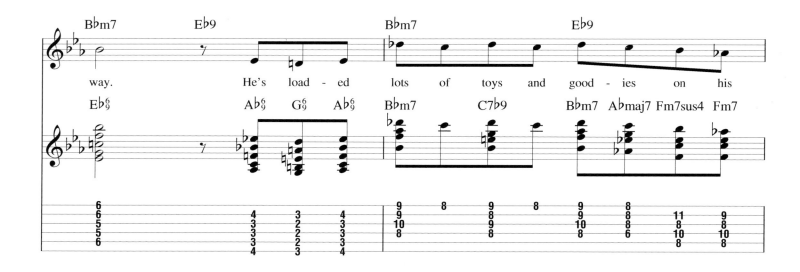

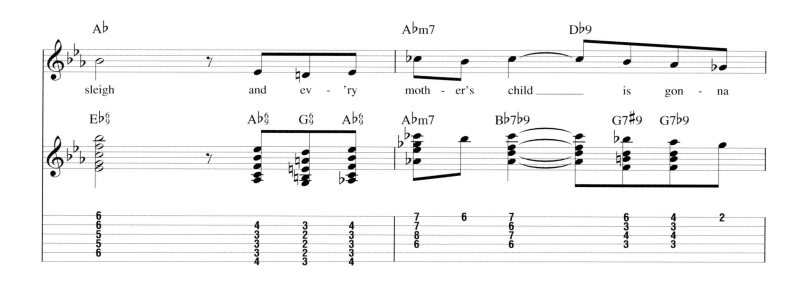

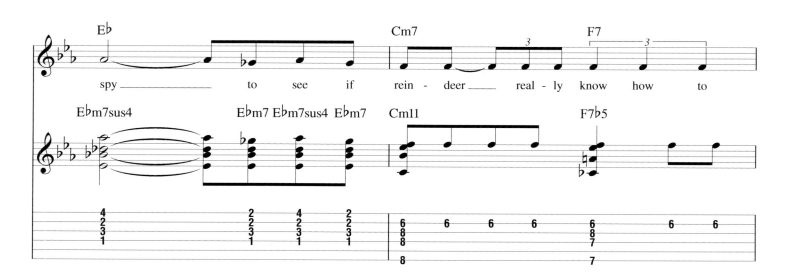

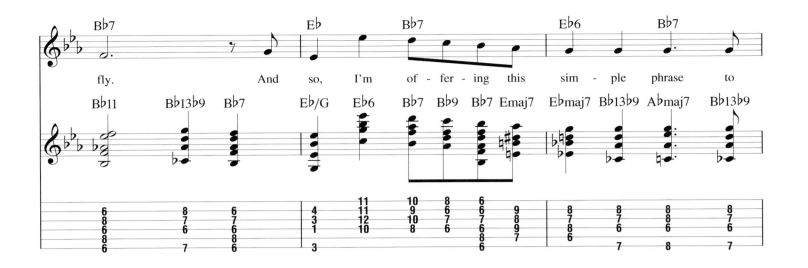

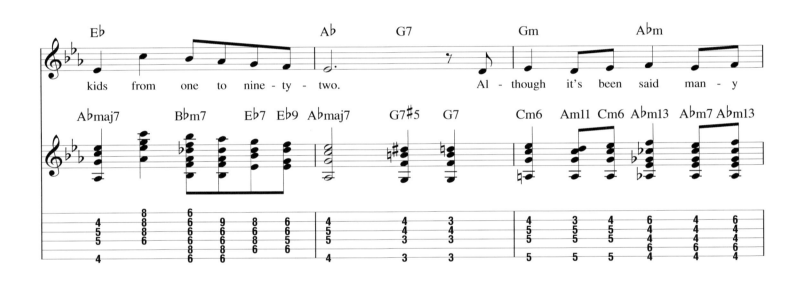

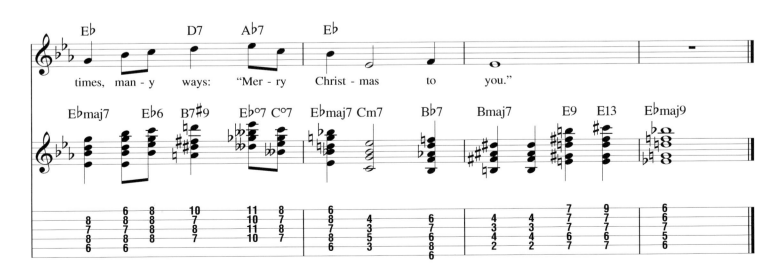

Come Sunday

By Duke Ellington

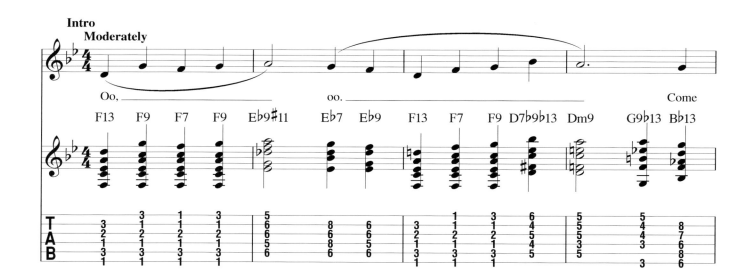

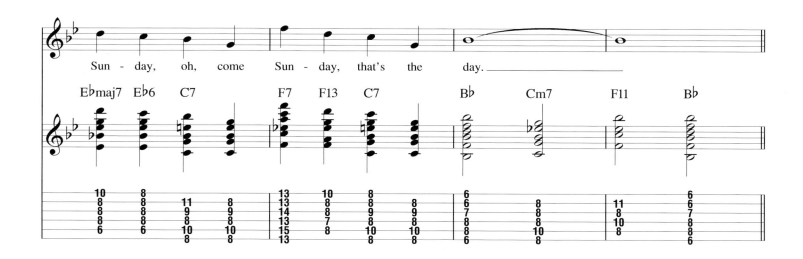

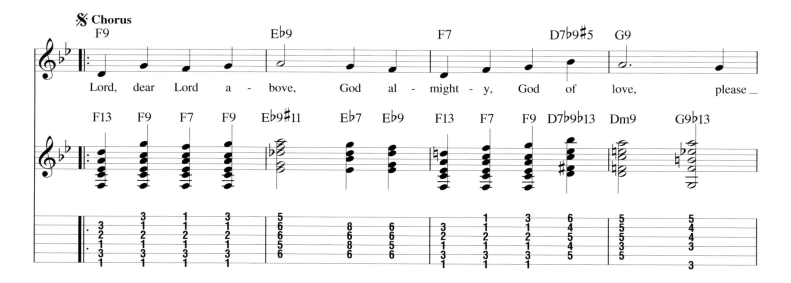

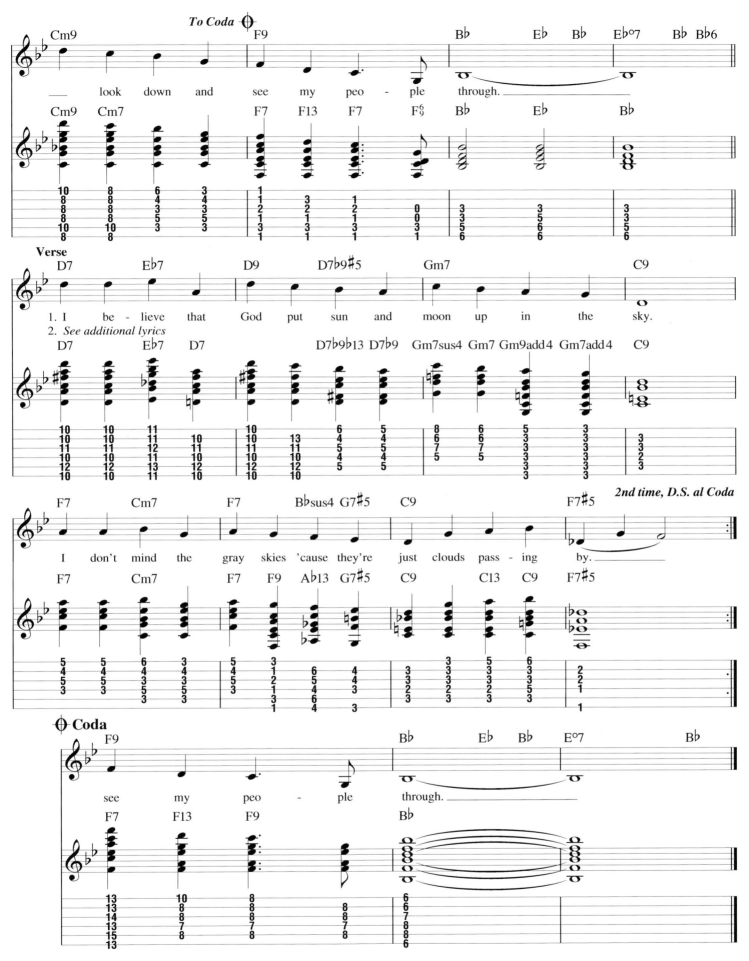

Additional Lyrics

2. I believe God is now, was then and always will be.
   With God's blessing we can make it through eternity.

East of the Sun (And West of the Moon)

Words and Music by Brooks Bowman

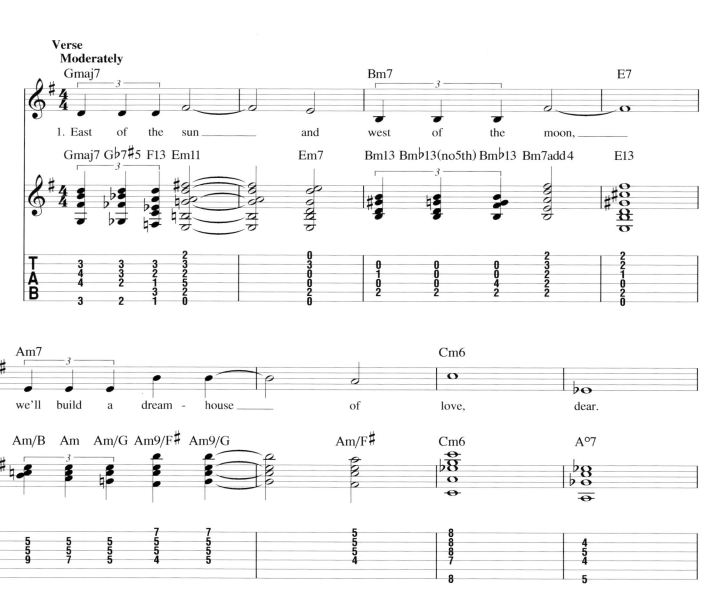

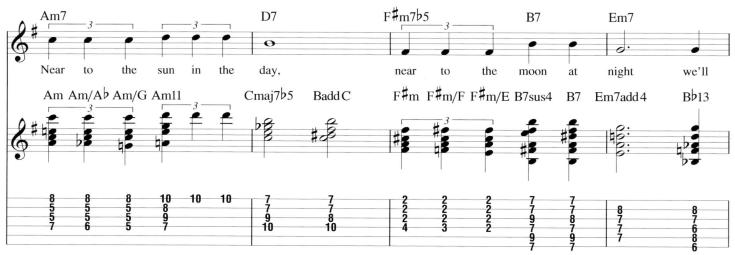

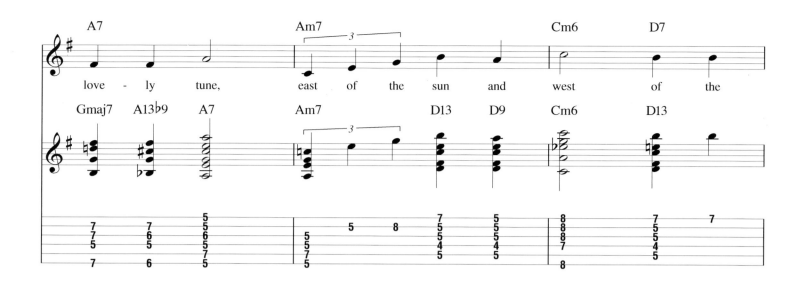

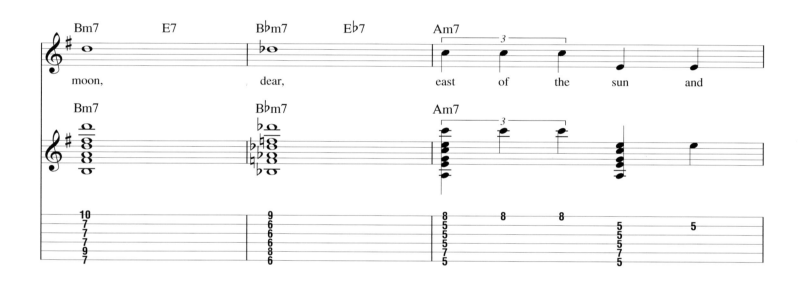

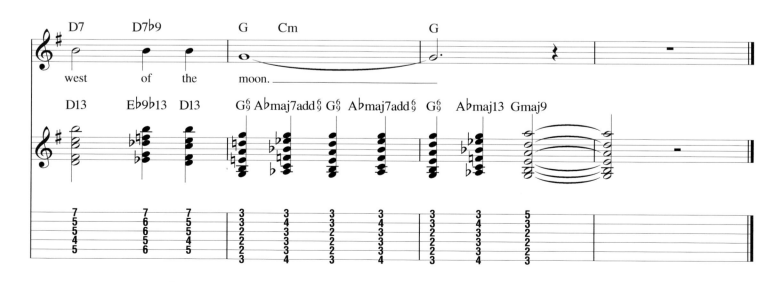

Ev'ry Time We Say Goodbye

Words and Music by Cole Porter

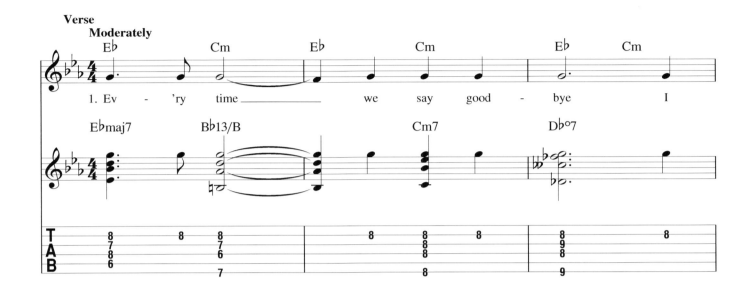

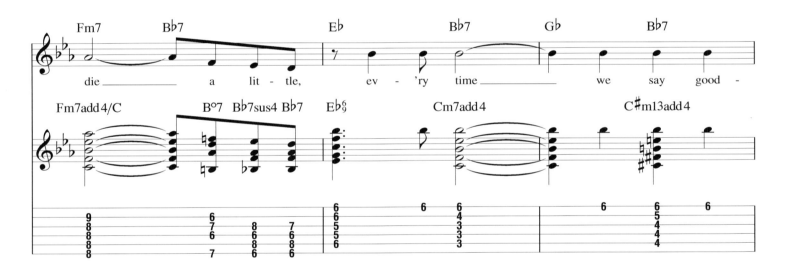

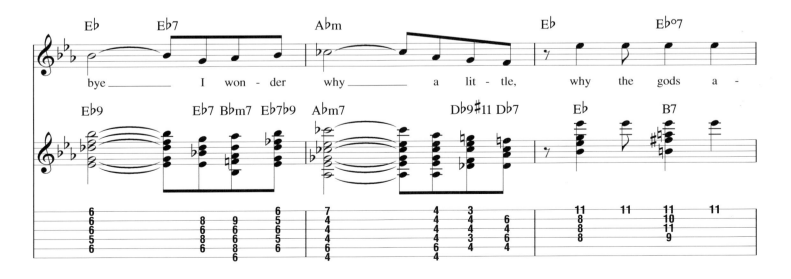

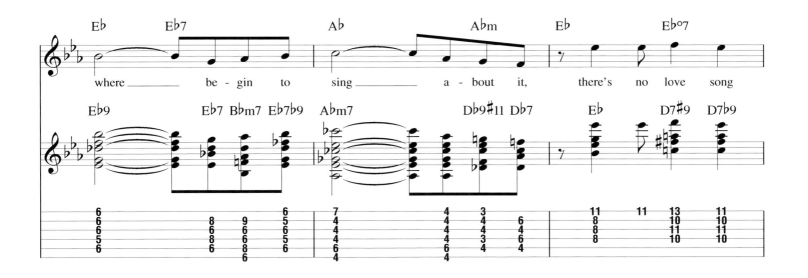

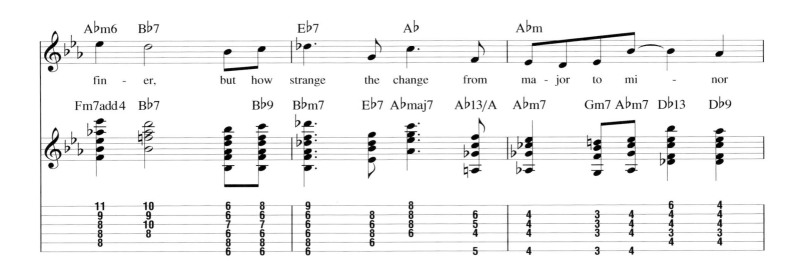

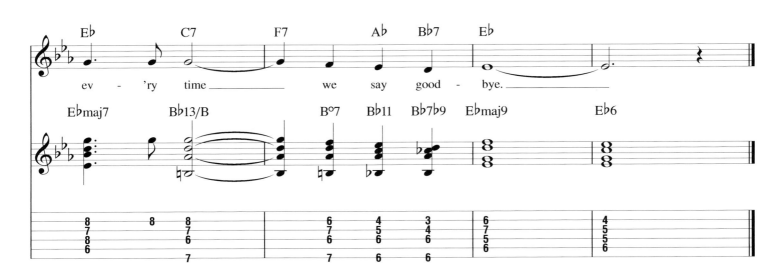

For All We Know

Words by Sam M. Lewis
Music by J. Fred Coots

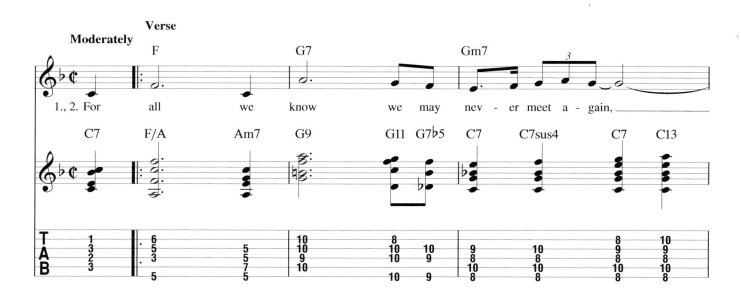

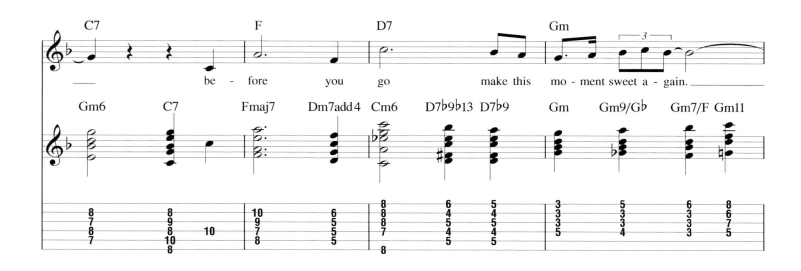

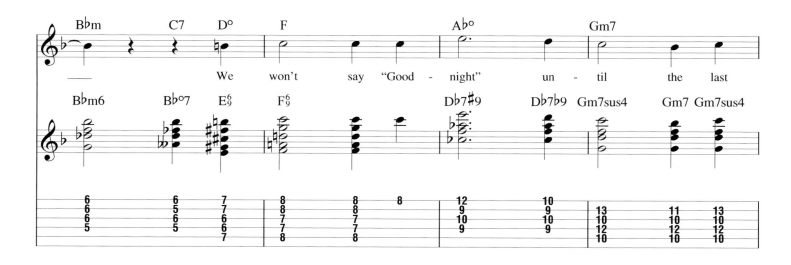

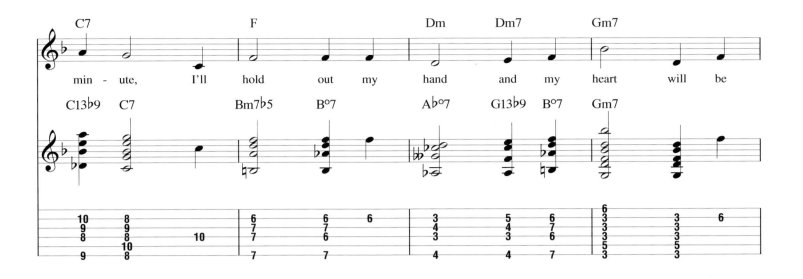

min - ute, I'll hold out my hand and my heart will be

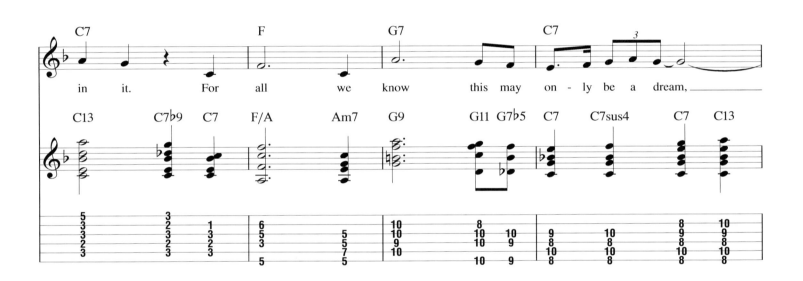

in it. For all we know this may on - ly be a dream,

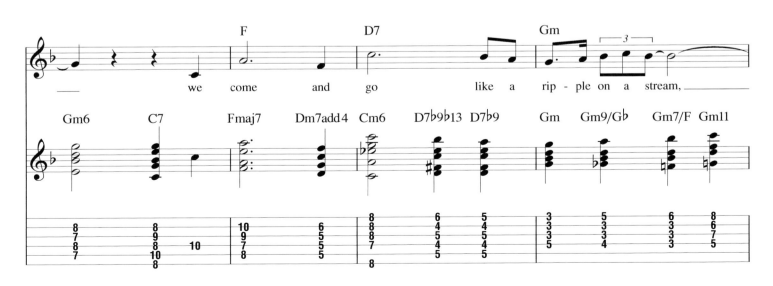

we come and go like a rip - ple on a stream,

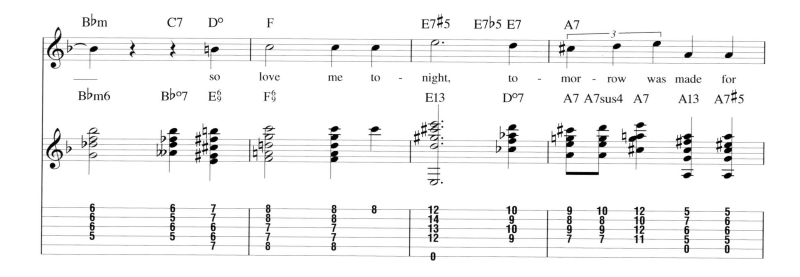

so love me to - night, to - mor - row was made for

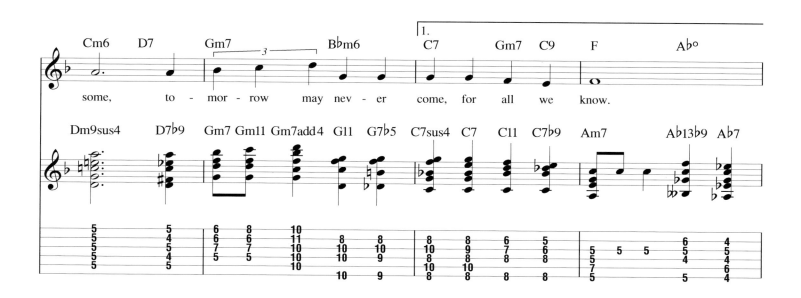

some, to - mor - row may nev - er come, for all we know.

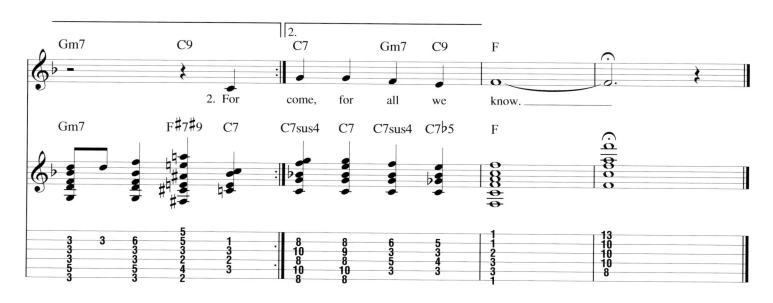

2. For come, for all we know.

How Insensitive
(Insensatez)

Music by Antonio Carlos Jobim
Original Words by Vinicius de Moraes
English Words by Norman Gimbel

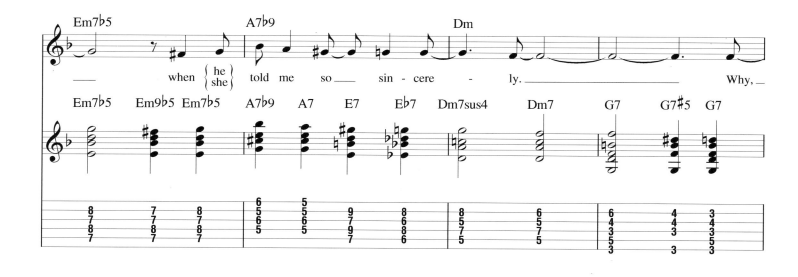

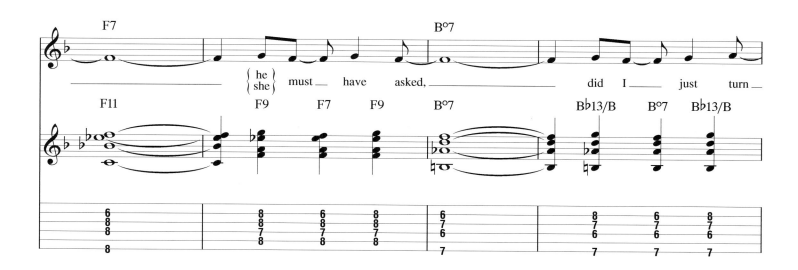

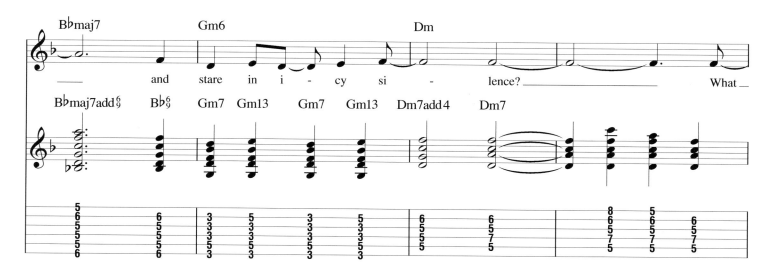

Additional Lyrics

2. Now {he's / she's} gone away
   And I'm alone with the memory of {his / her} last look.
   Vague and drawn and sad.
   I see it still, all {his / her} heartbreak in that last look.
   How, {he / she} must have asked,
   Could I just turn and stare in icy silence?
   What was I to do?
   What can one do when a love affair is over?

Four

By Miles Davis

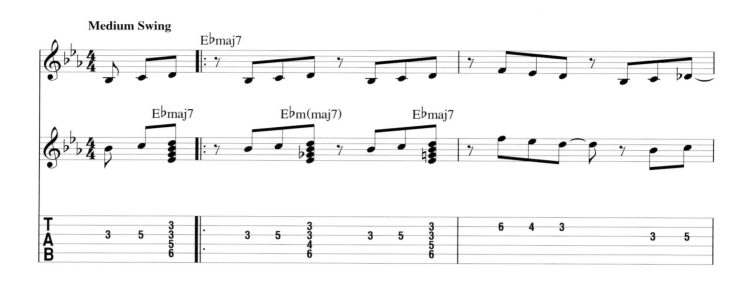

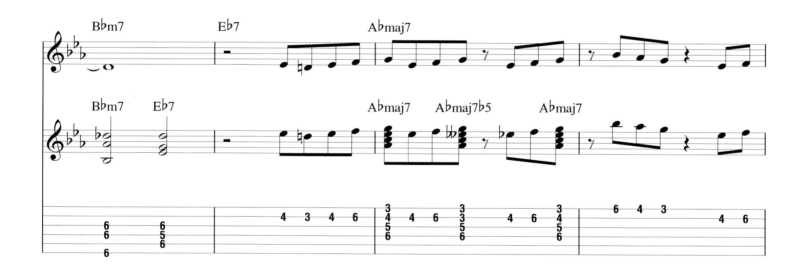

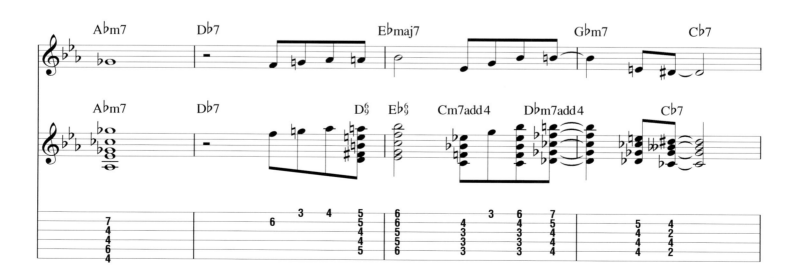

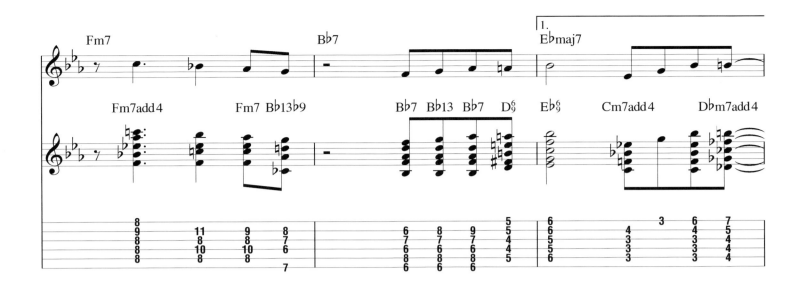

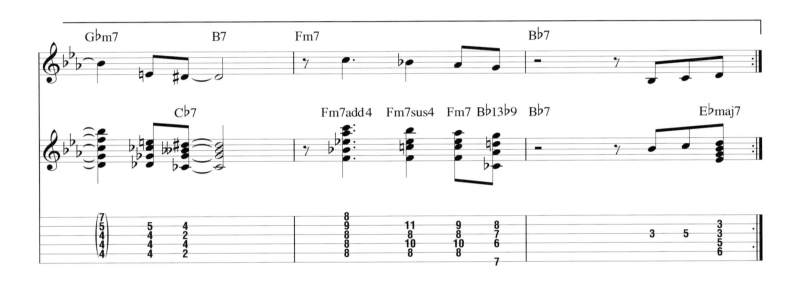

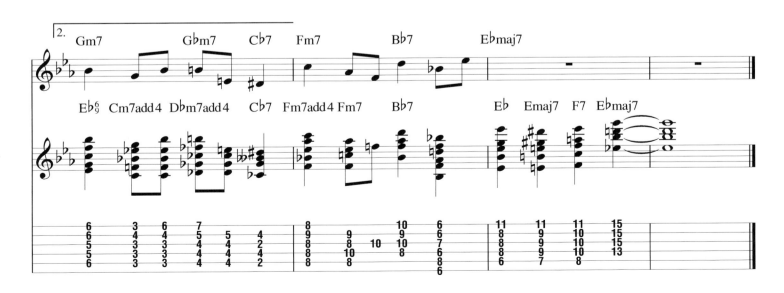

I Get Along Without You Very Well
(Except Sometimes)

Words and Music by Hoagy Carmichael
Inspired by a poem written by J.B. Thompson

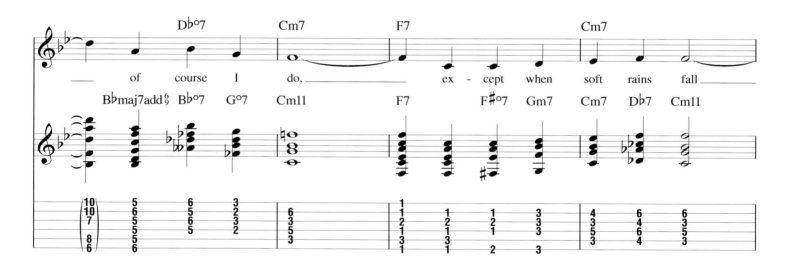

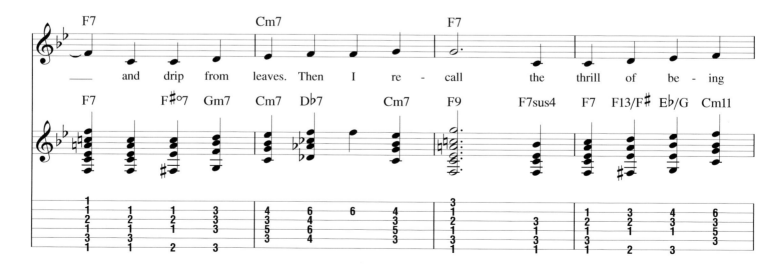

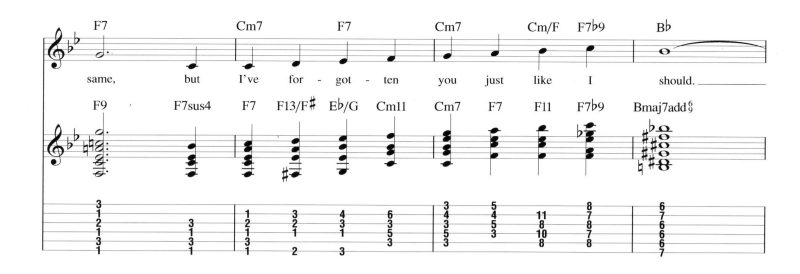

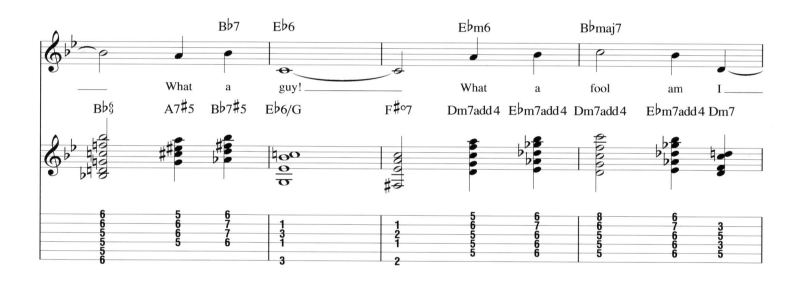

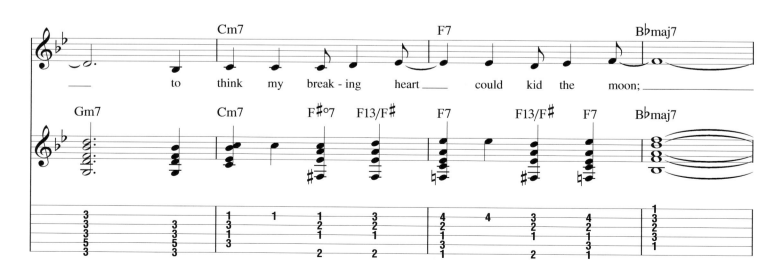

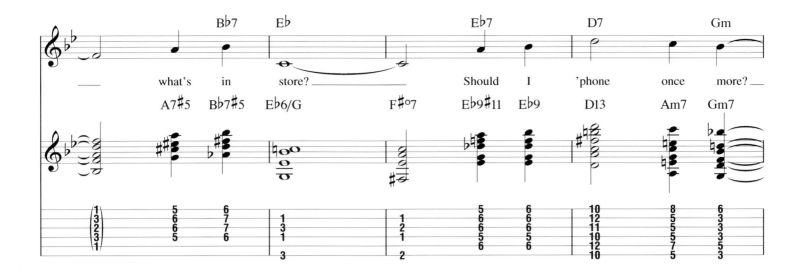

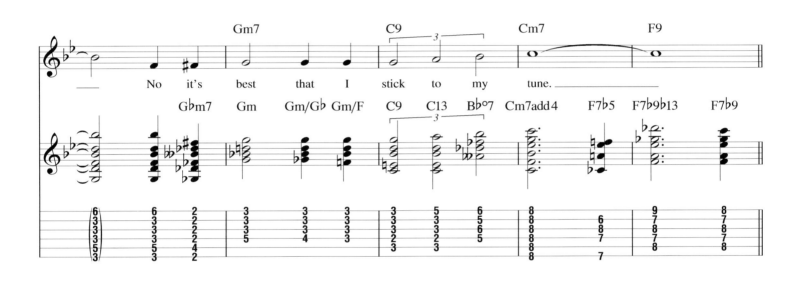

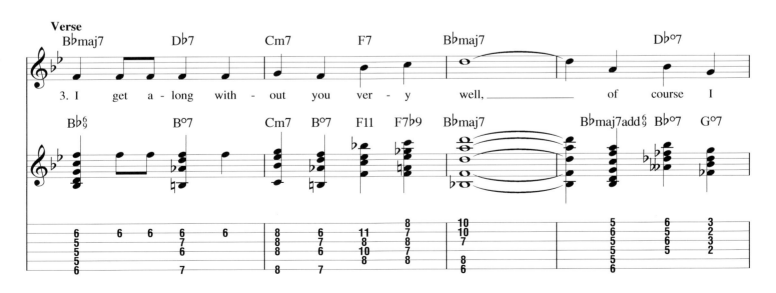

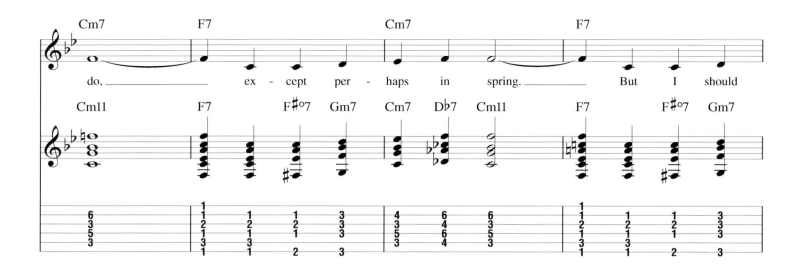

do, _____ ex - cept per - haps in spring. _____ But I should

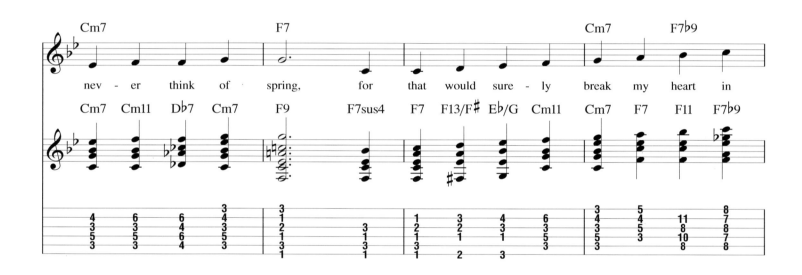

nev - er think of spring, for that would sure - ly break my heart in

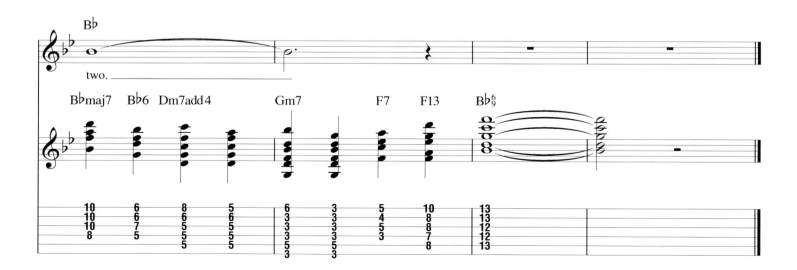

two. _____

I Remember Clifford

By Benny Golson

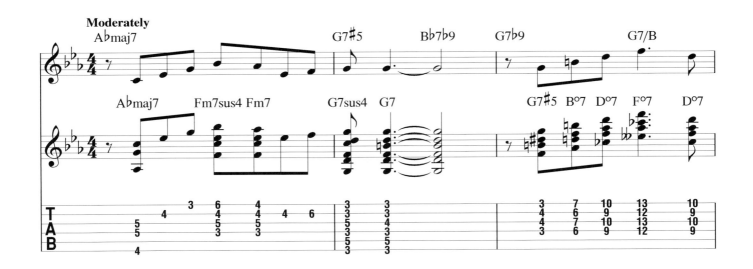

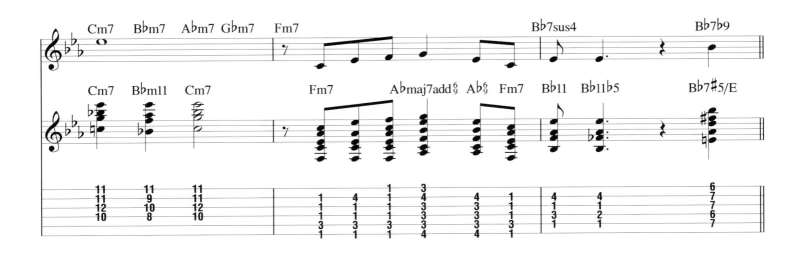

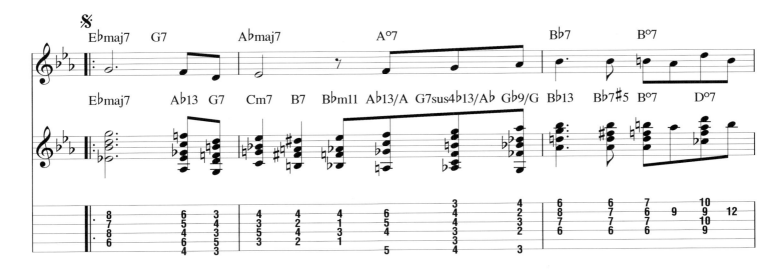

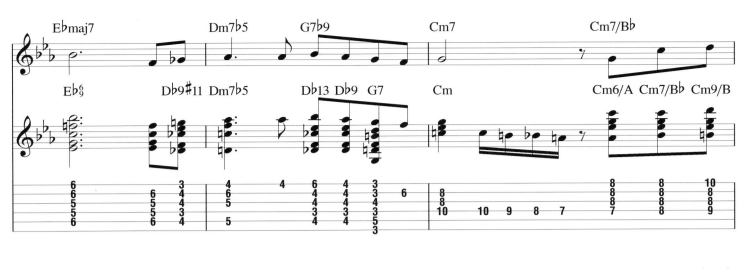

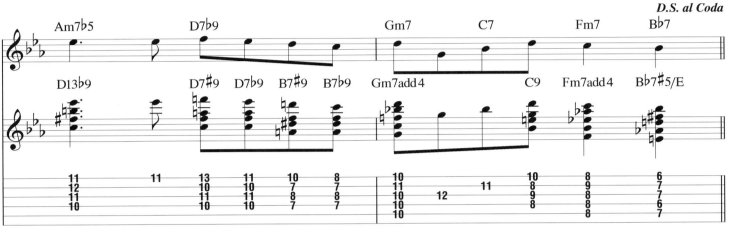

D.S. al Coda

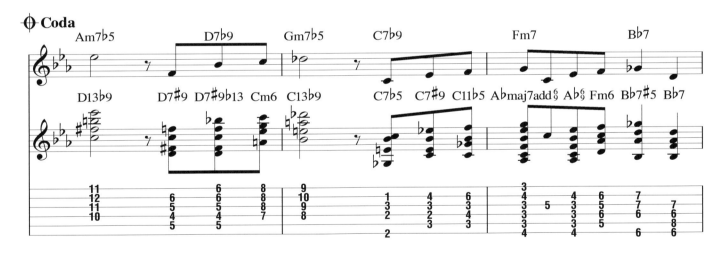

$\oplus$ **Coda**

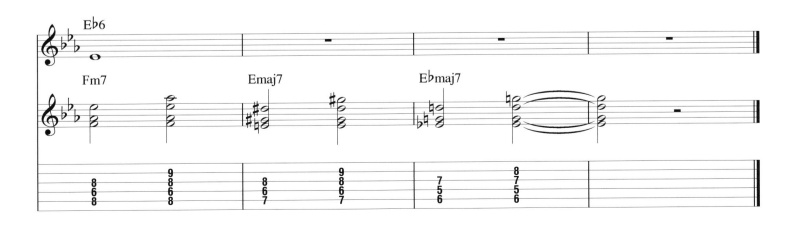

I Should Care

Words and Music by Sammy Cahn, Paul Weston and Axel Stordahl

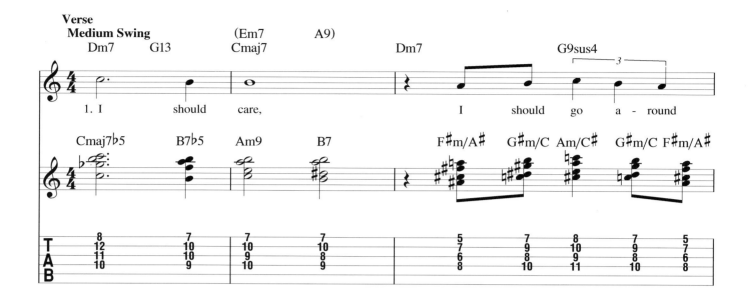

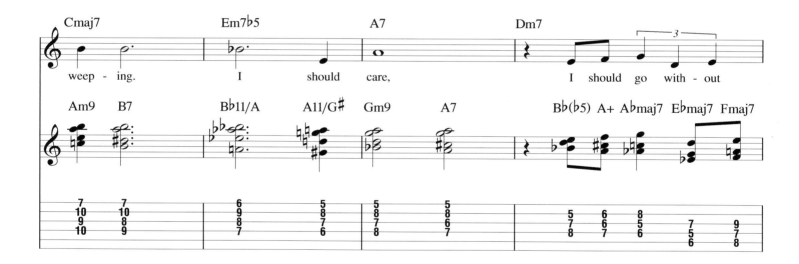

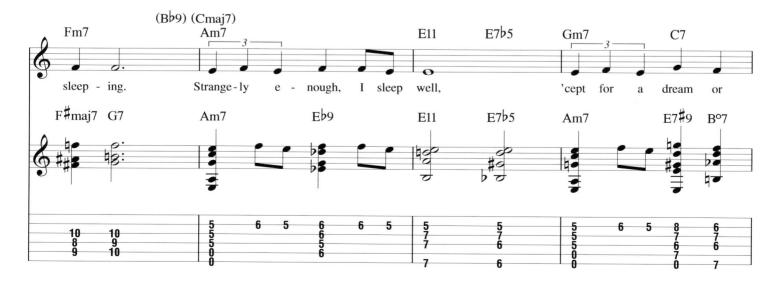

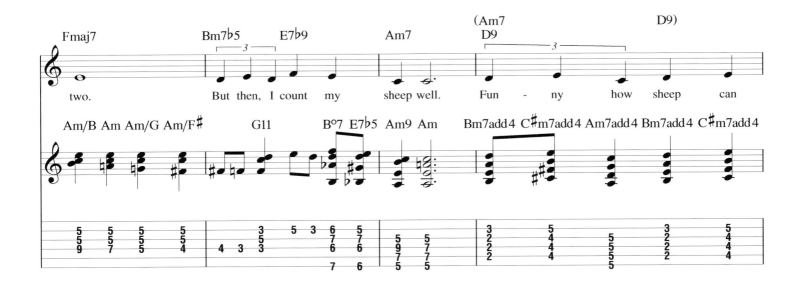

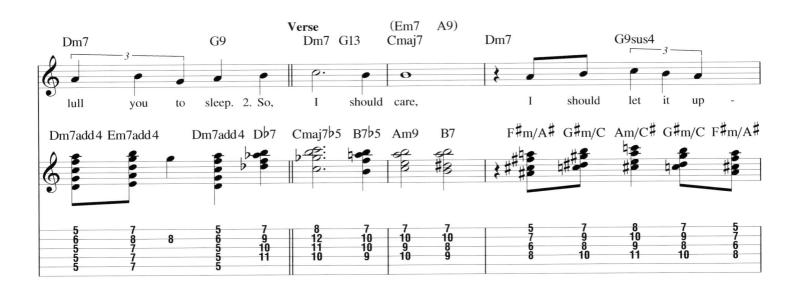

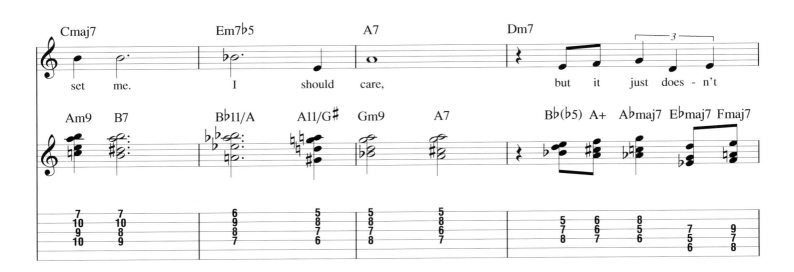

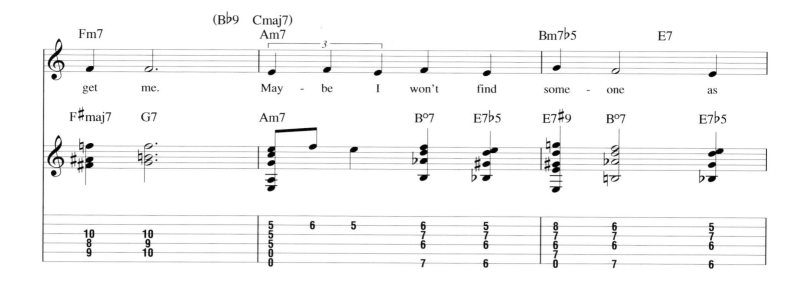

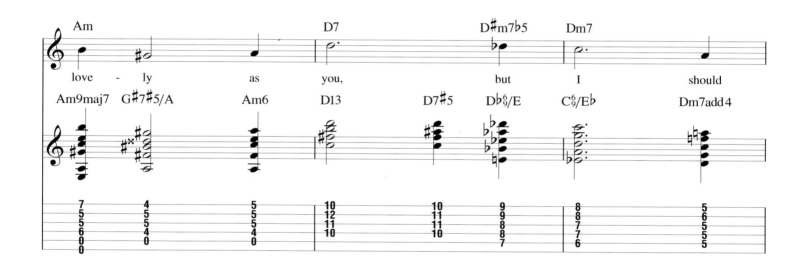

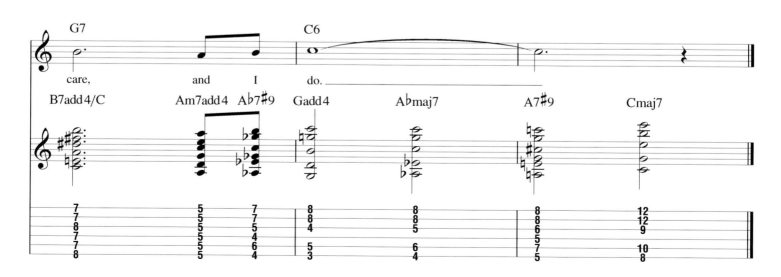

I've Got the World on a String

Lyric by Ted Koehler
Music by Harold Arlen

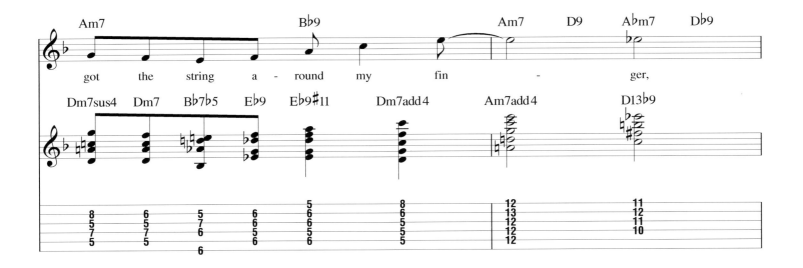

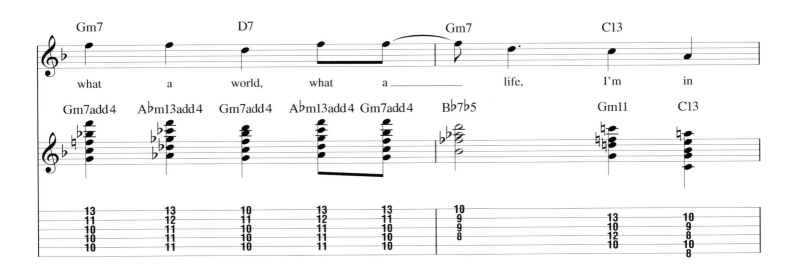

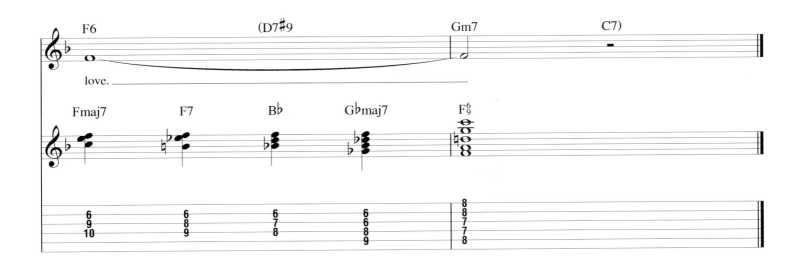

Additional Lyrics

2. I've got a song that I sing,
   I can make the rain go,
   Any time I move my finger.
   Lucky me, can't you see, I'm in love.

It's Only a Paper Moon

Lyric by Billy Rose and E.Y. Harburg
Music by Harold Arlen

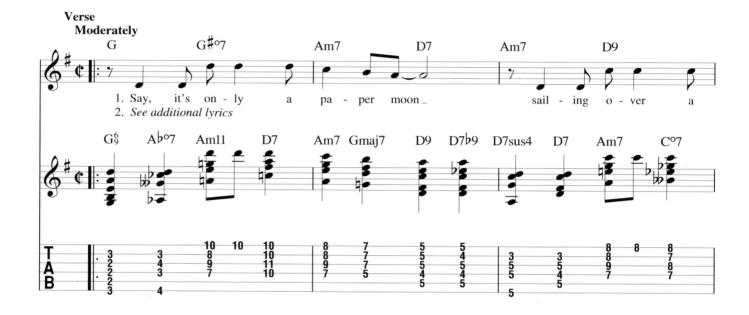

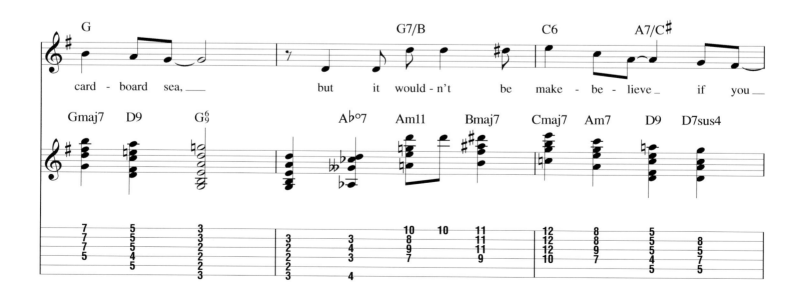

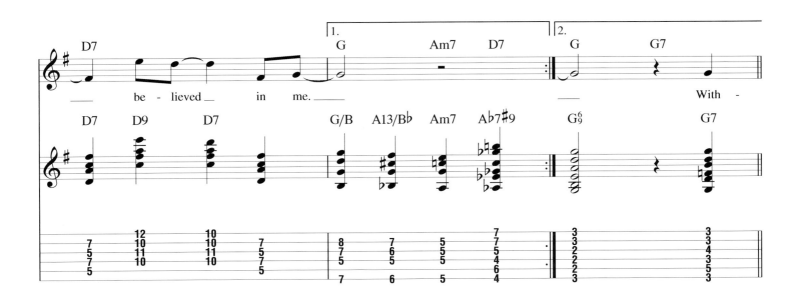

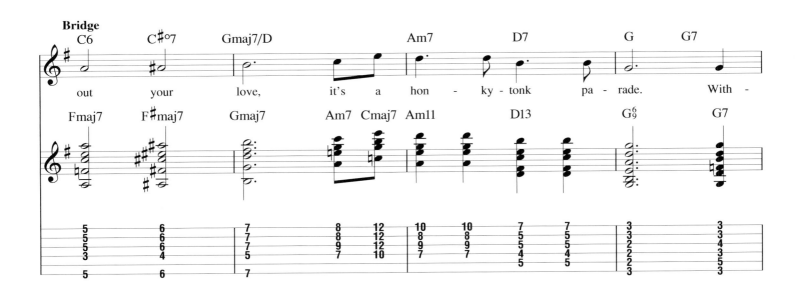

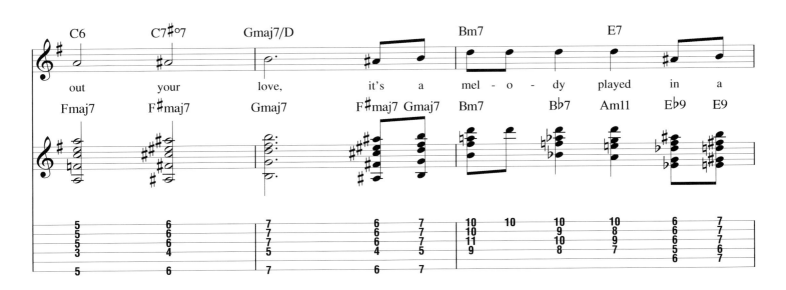

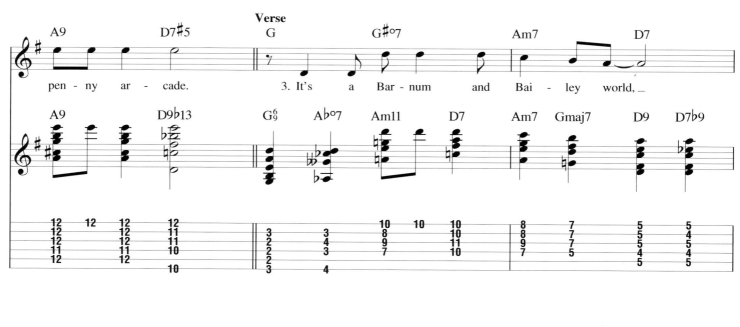

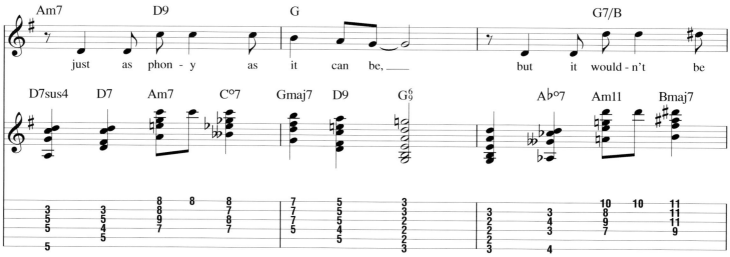

Additional Lyrics

2. Yes, it's only a canvas sky
   Hanging over a muslin tree,
   But it wouldn't be make believe,
   If you believed in me.

It's You or No One

Words by Sammy Cahn
Music by Jule Styne

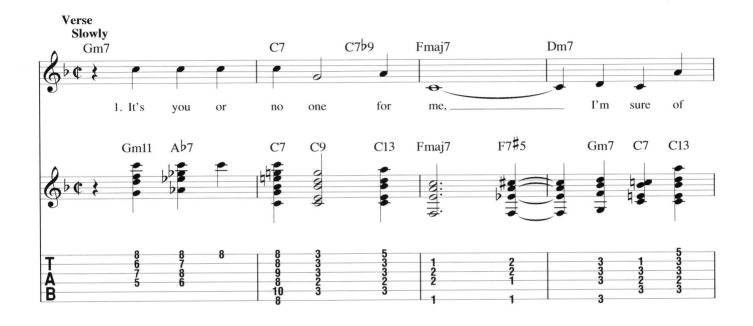

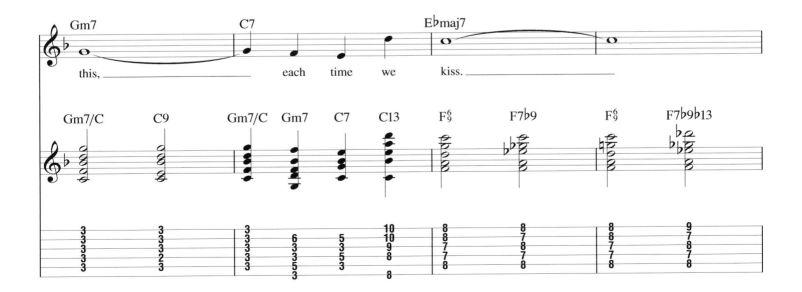

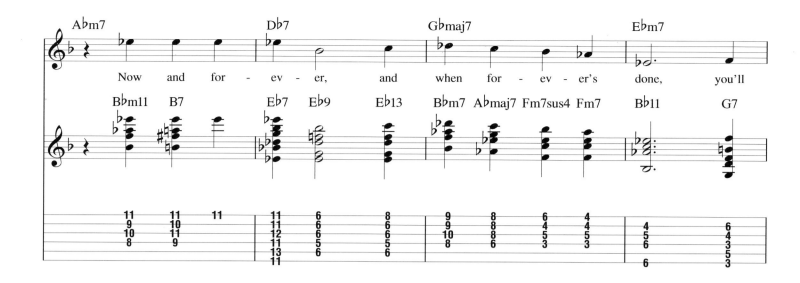

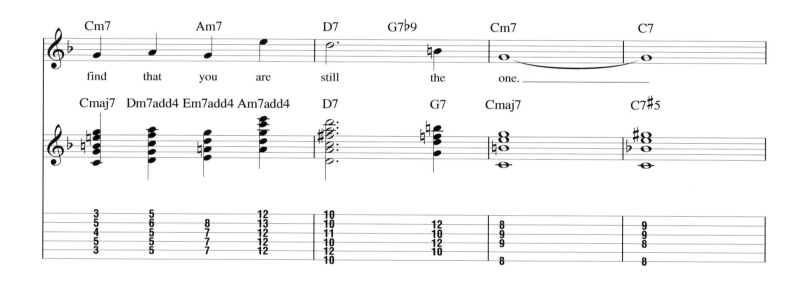

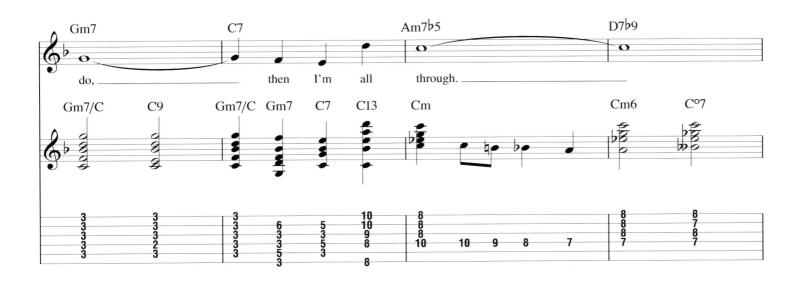

do, _____ then I'm all through. _____

There's this a - bout you, my world's an emp - ty world with - out you,

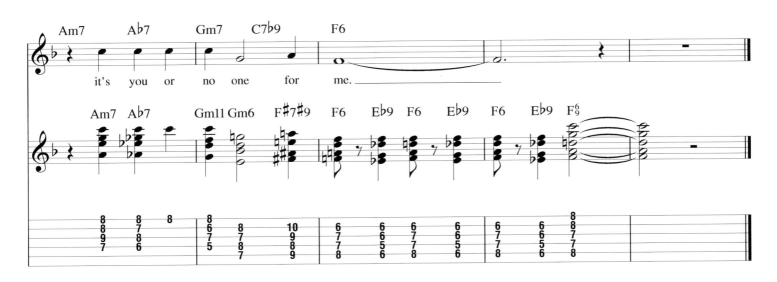

it's you or no one for me. _____

Lament

By J.J. Johnson

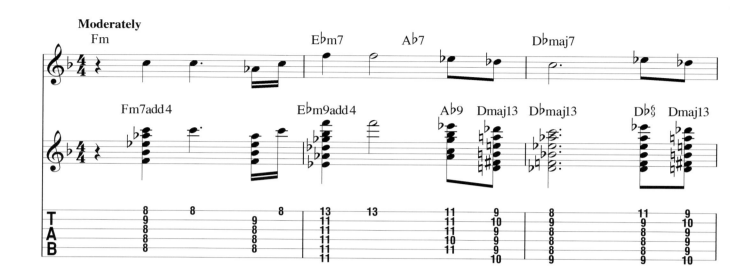

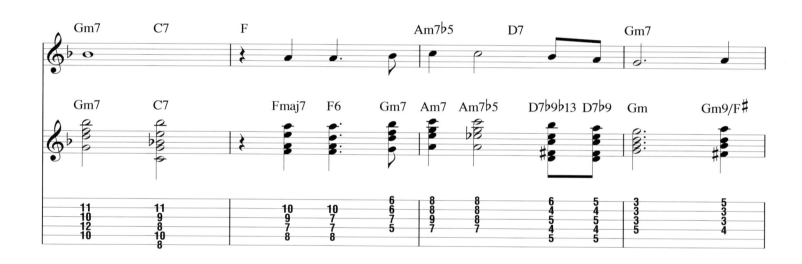

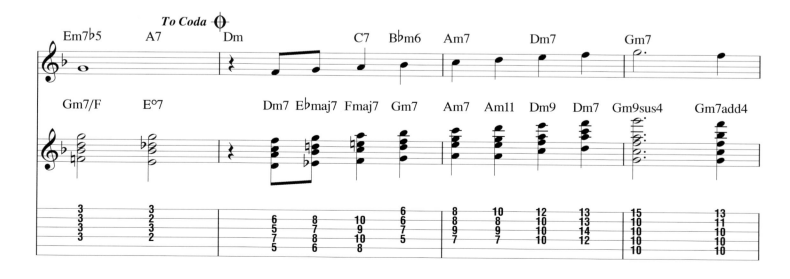

69

Last Night When We Were Young

Lyric by E.Y. Harburg
Music by Harold Arlen

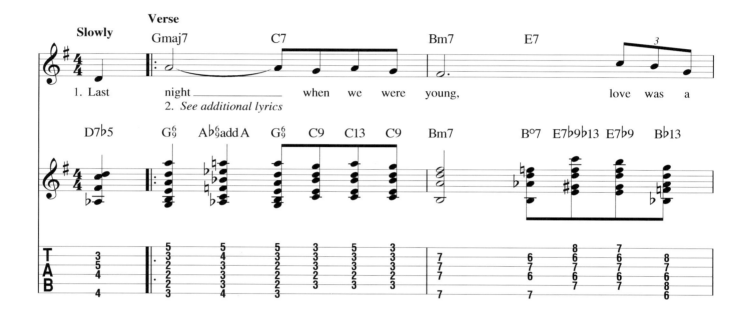

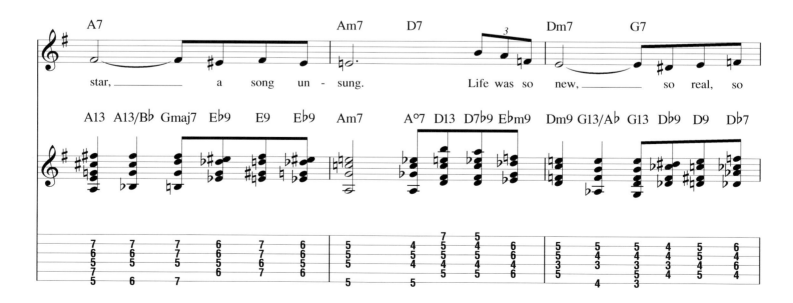

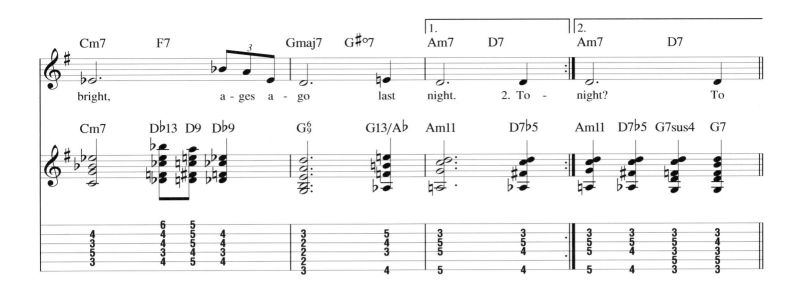

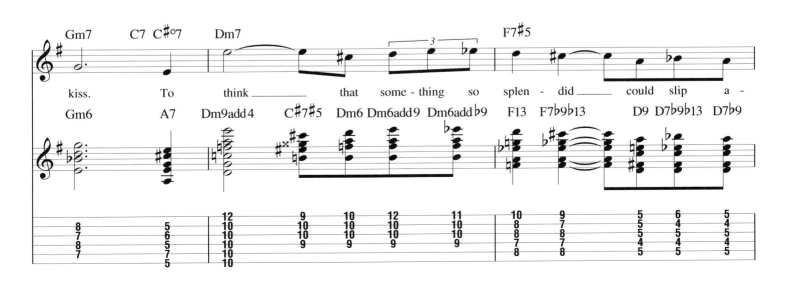

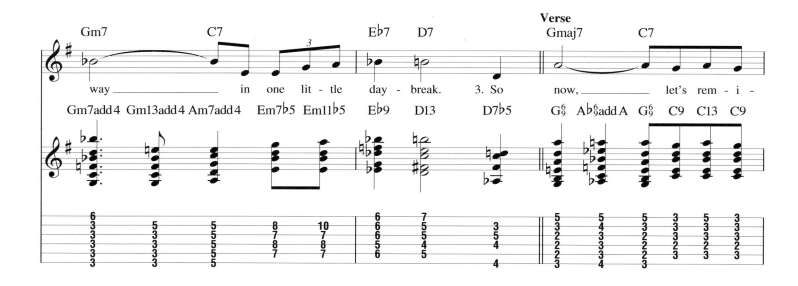

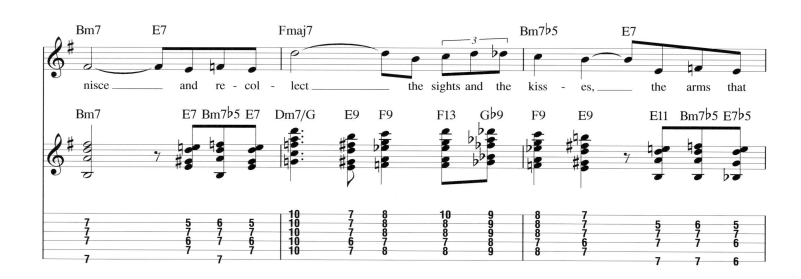

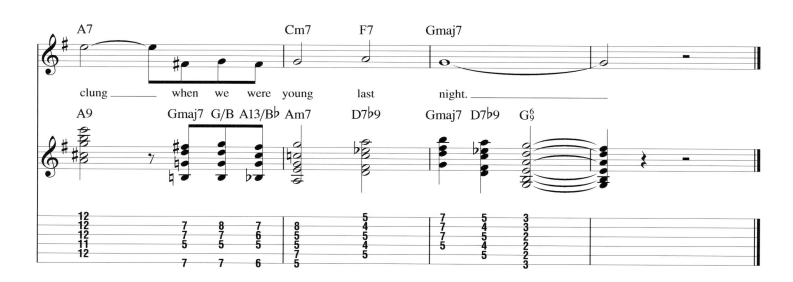

Additional Lyrics

2. Today the world is old,
   You flew away and time grew cold.
   Where is that star that seemed so bright,
   Ages ago last night?

Manhã de Carnaval
(A Day in the Life of a Fool)

Words by Carl Sigman
Music by Luiz Bonfa

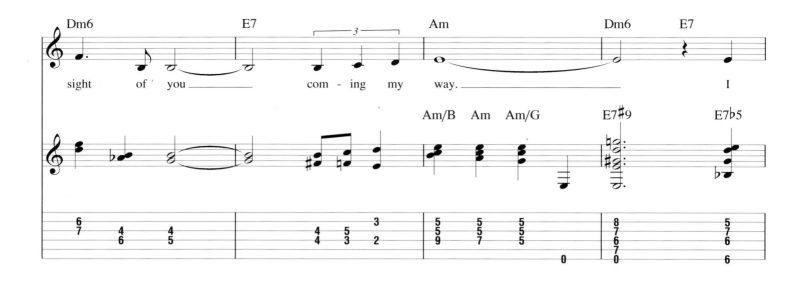

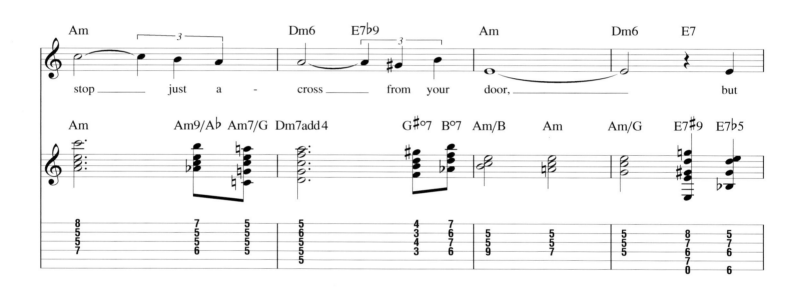

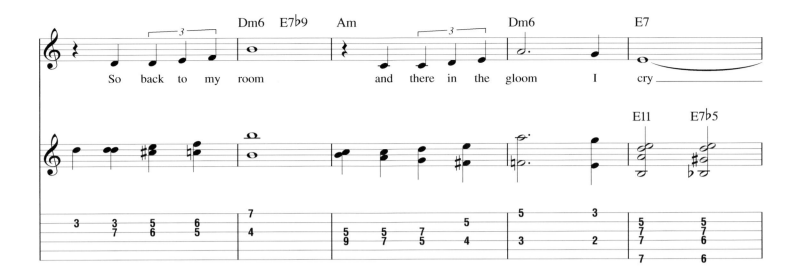

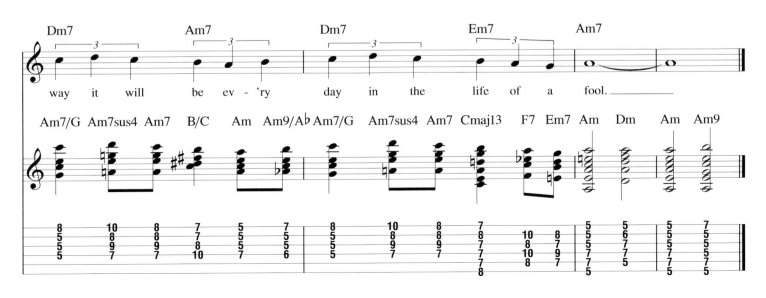

Meditation
(Meditacáo)

Music by Antonio Carlos Jobim
Original Words by Newton Mendonca
English Words by Norman Gimbel

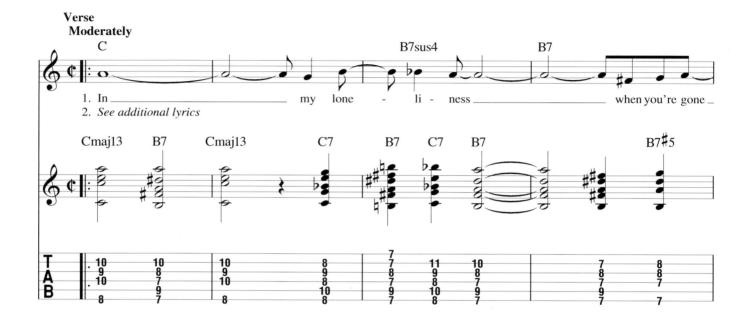

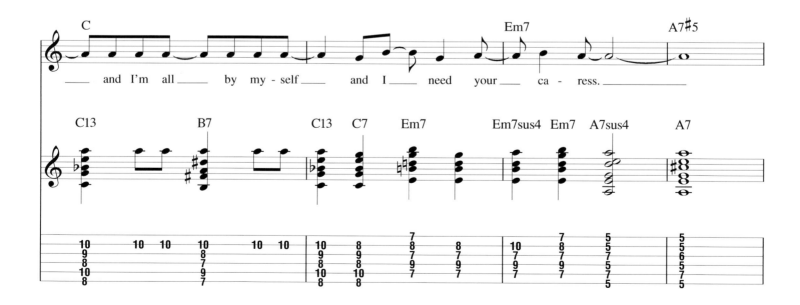

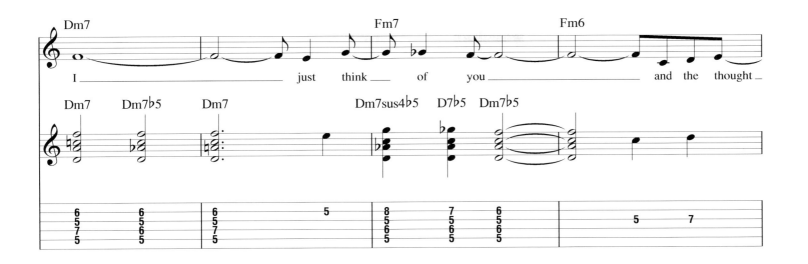

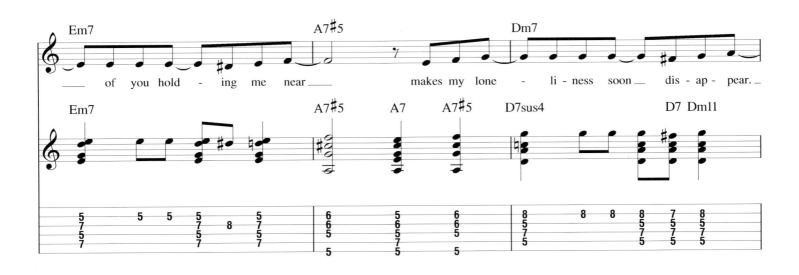

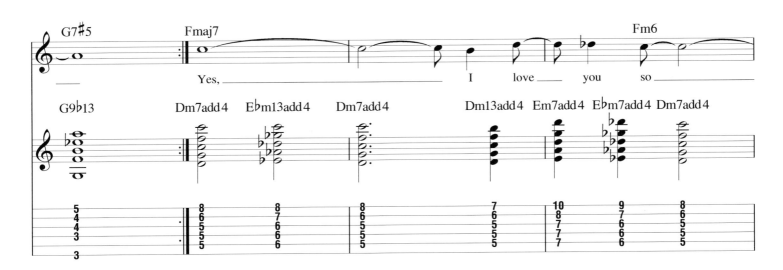

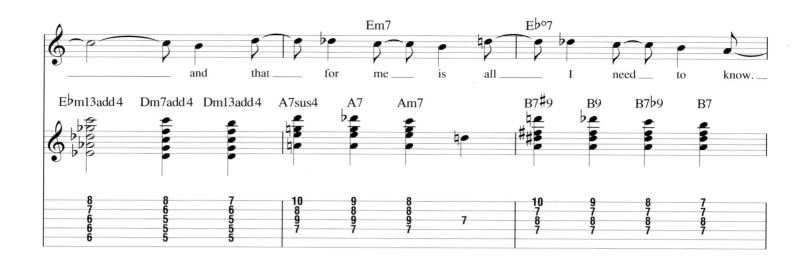

and that ____ for me ____ is all ____ I need ____ to know. ____

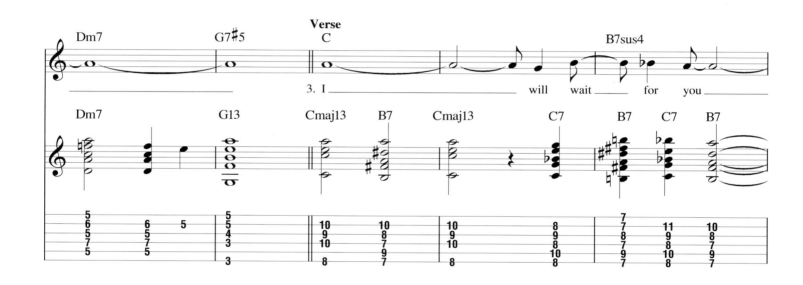

3. I ____ will wait ____ for you ____

'til the sun ____ falls from out ____ of the sky ____ for what ____ else can

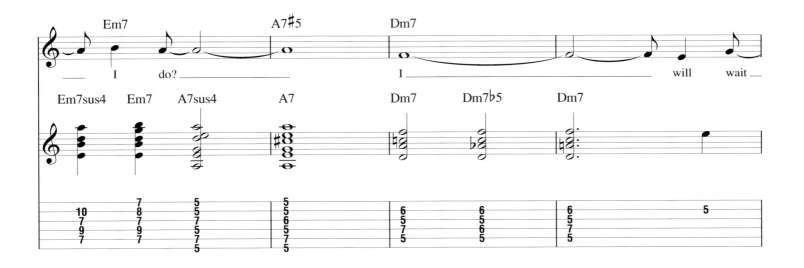

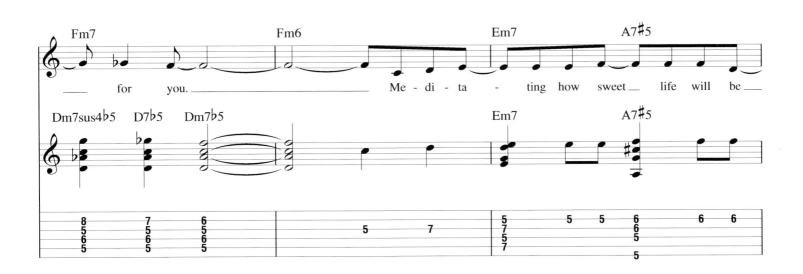

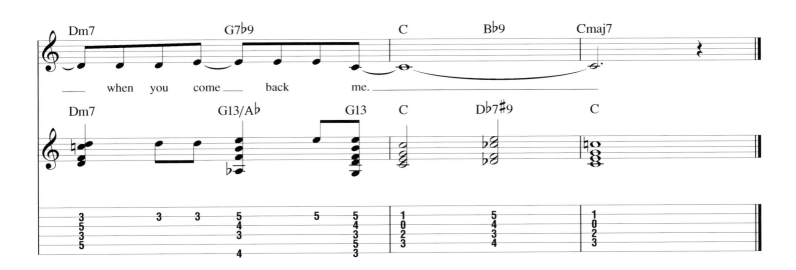

Additional Lyrics

2. Though you're far away,
   I have only to close my eyes and you are back to stay.
   I just close my eyes,
   And the sadness that missing you brings
   Is gone and this heart of mine sings.

Mercy, Mercy, Mercy

Composed by Josef Zawinul

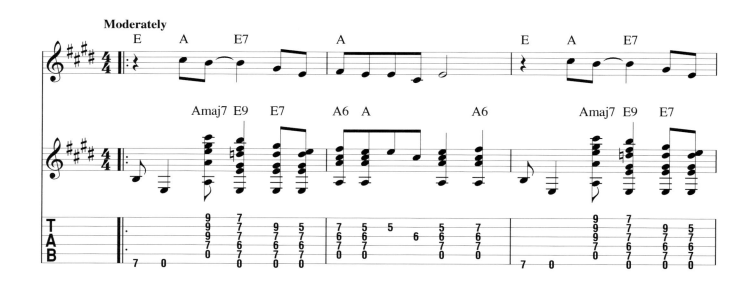

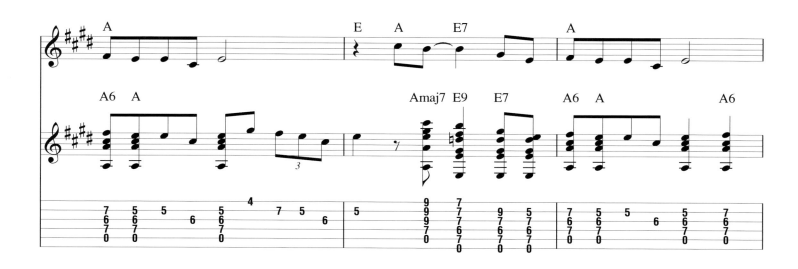

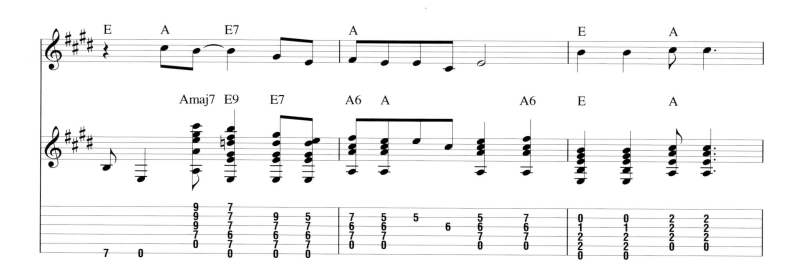

Moonlight Becomes You

Words by Johnny Burke
Music by James Van Heusen

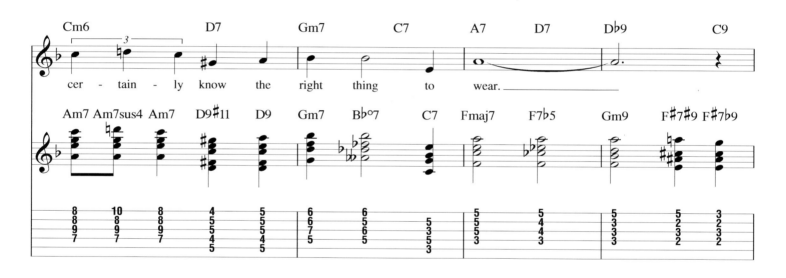

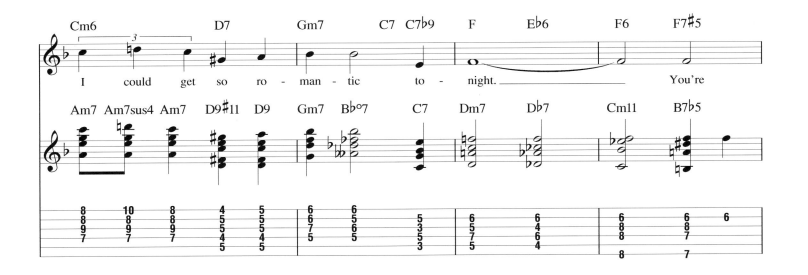

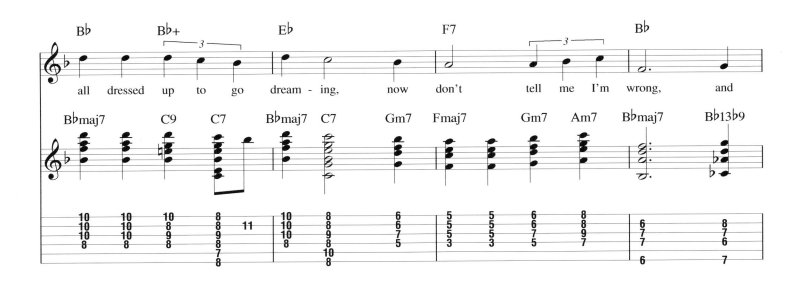

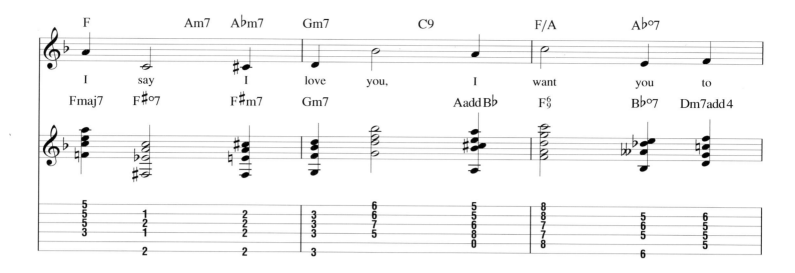

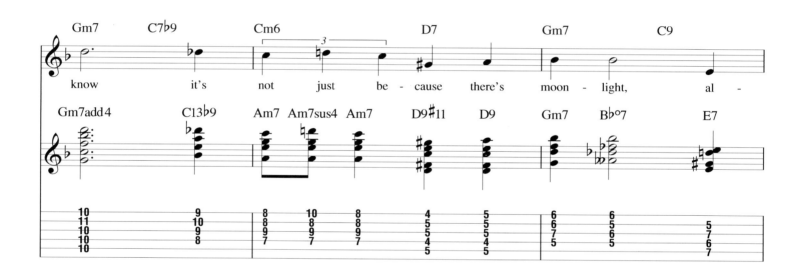

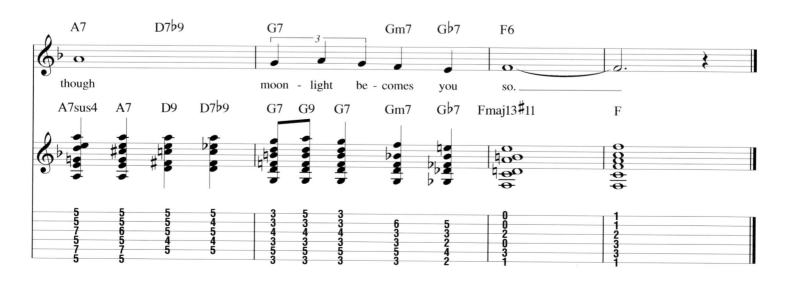

Poor Butterfly

Words by John L. Golden
Music by Raymond Hubbell

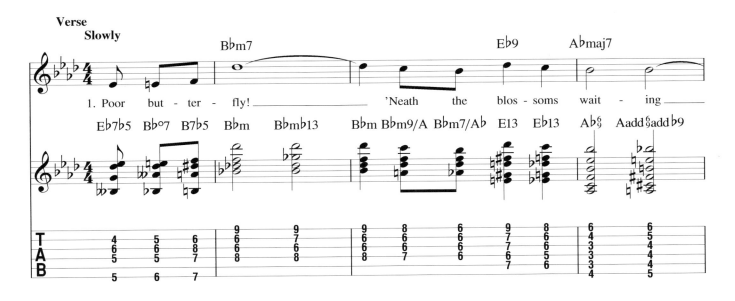

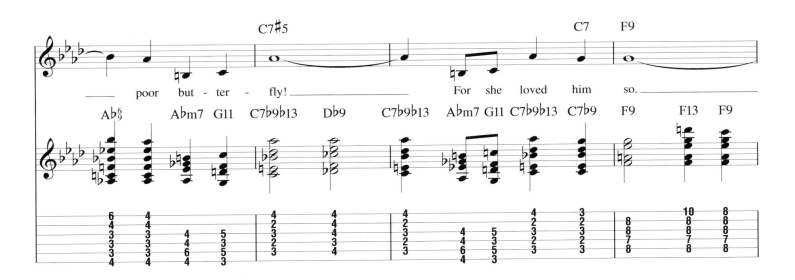

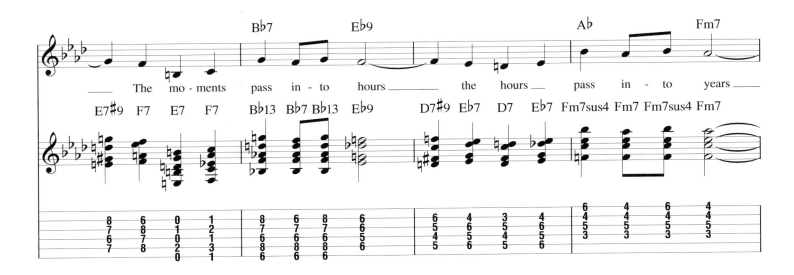

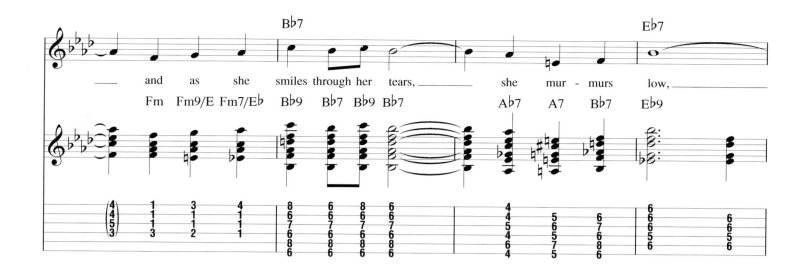

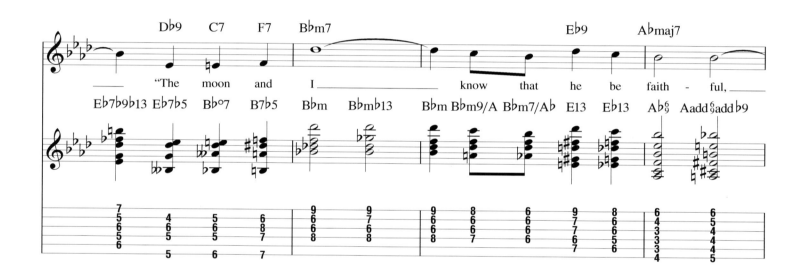

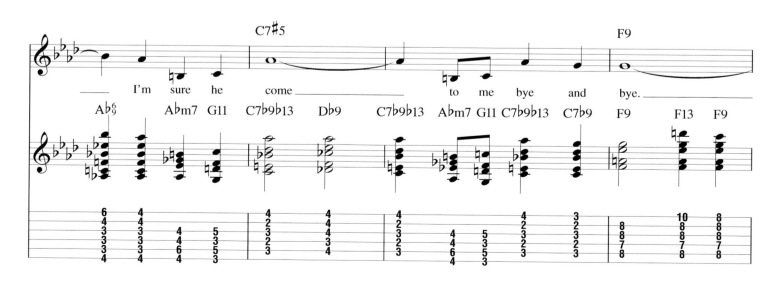

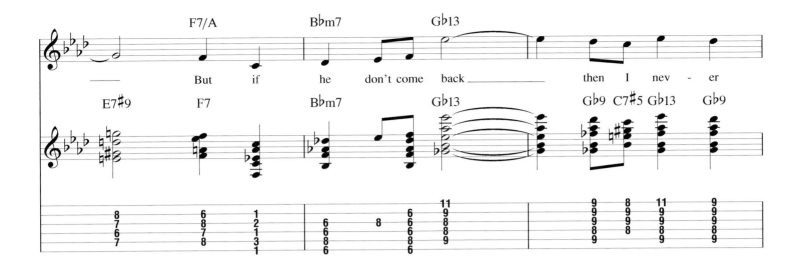

But if he don't come back _____ then I nev - er

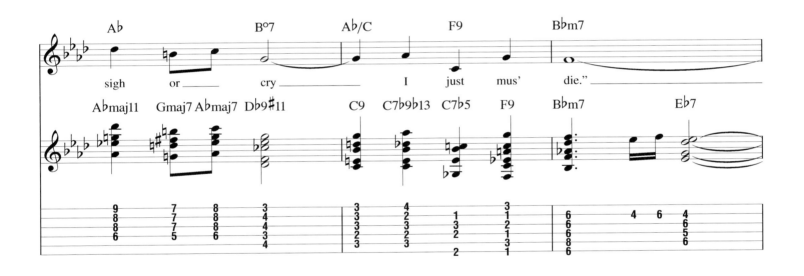

sigh or _____ cry _____ I just mus' die." _____

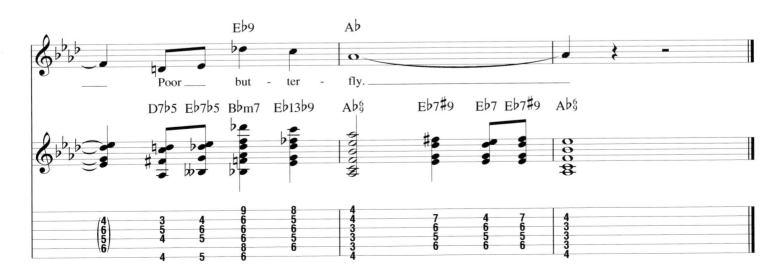

_____ Poor _____ but - ter - fly.

Stompin' at the Savoy

Words and Music by Benny Goodman, Edgar Sampson, Chick Webb and Andy Razaf

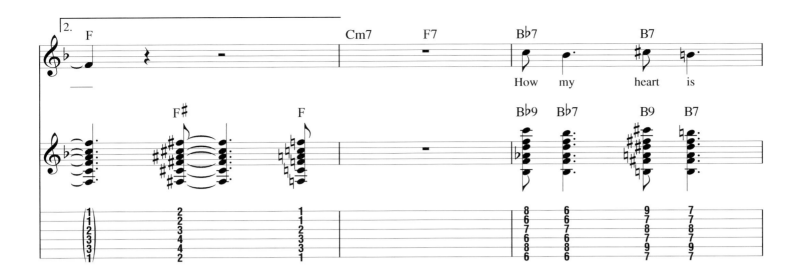

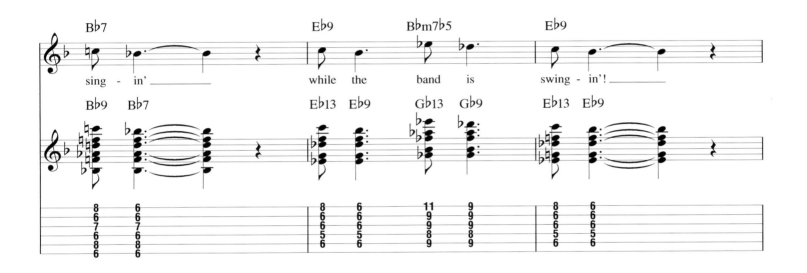

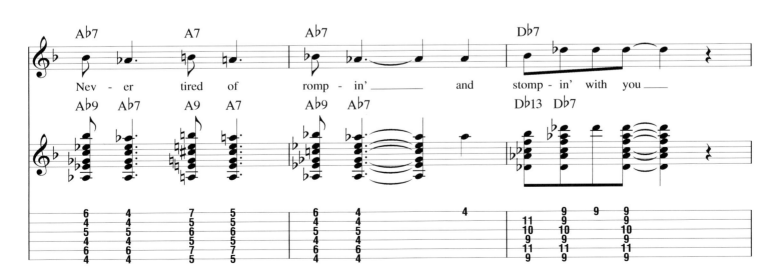

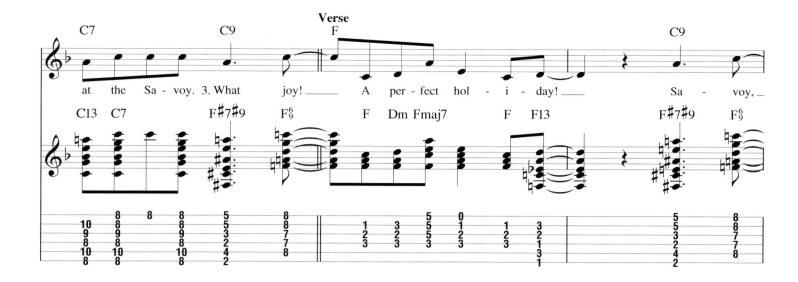

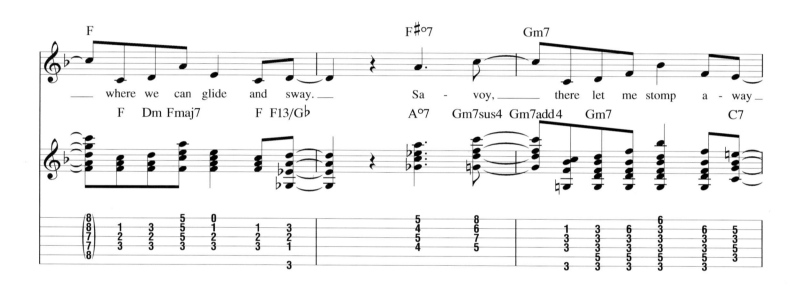

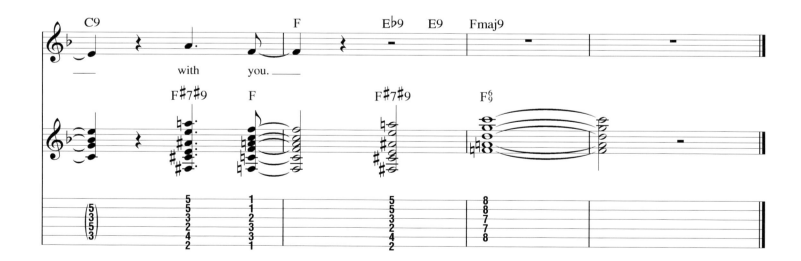

Additional Lyrics

2. Your form, just like a clingin' vine;
Your lips so warm and sweet as wine.
Your cheek so soft and close to mine,
Divine!

This Is All I Ask
(Beautiful Girls Walk a Little Slower)

Words and Music by Gordon Jenkins

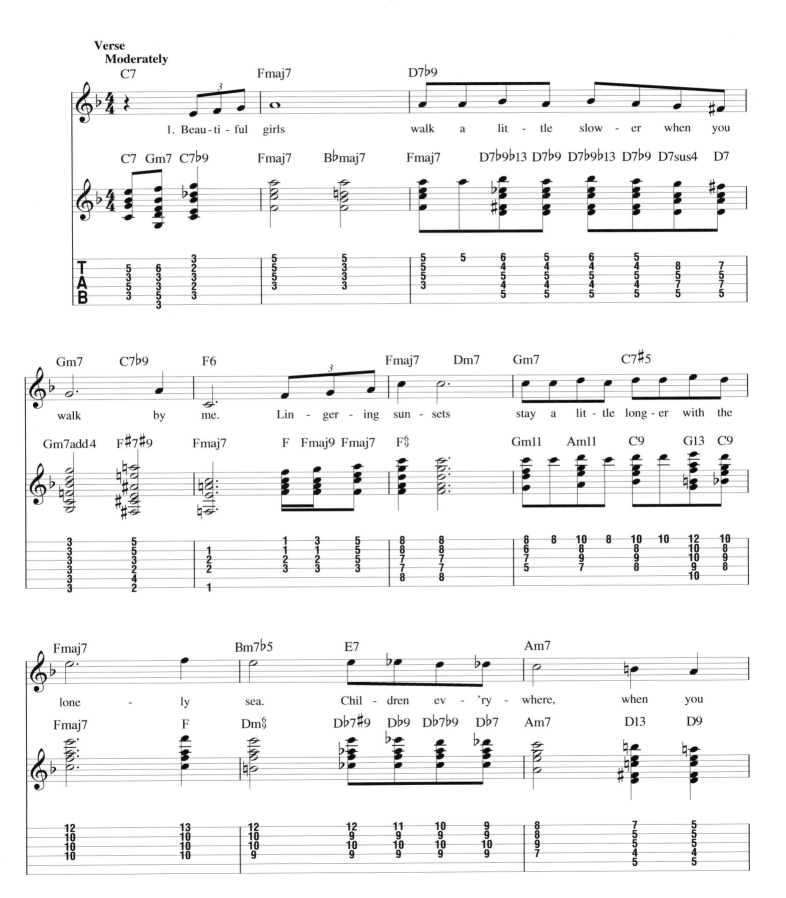

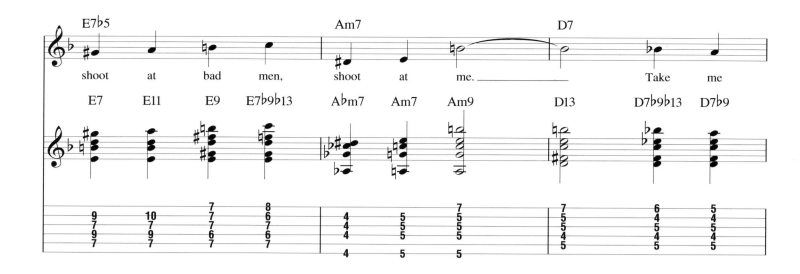

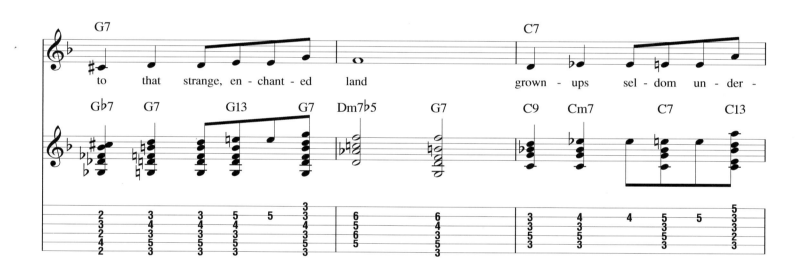

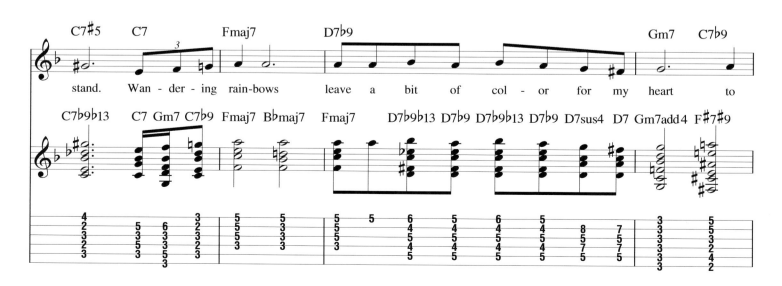

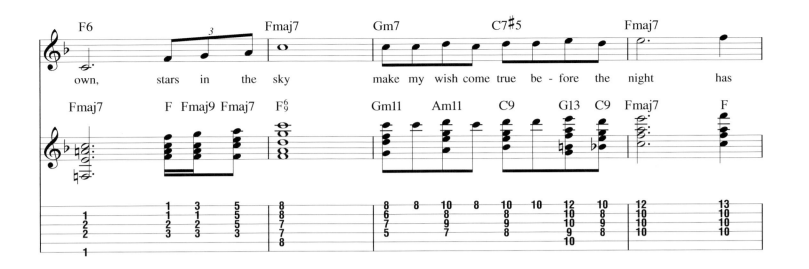

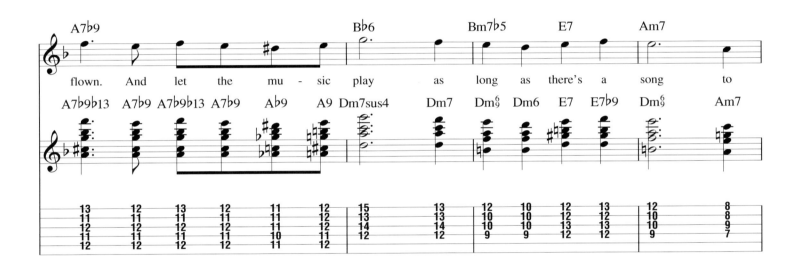

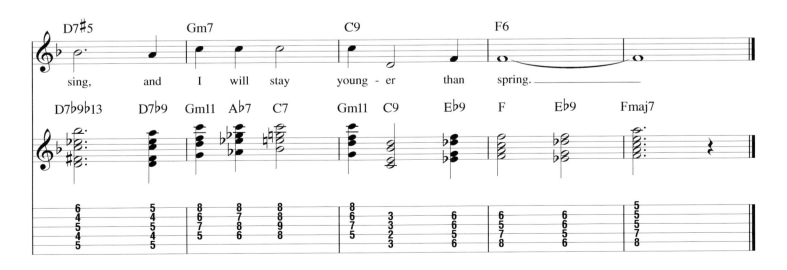

Sweet and Lovely

Words and Music by Gus Arnheim, Charles N. Daniels and Harry Tobias

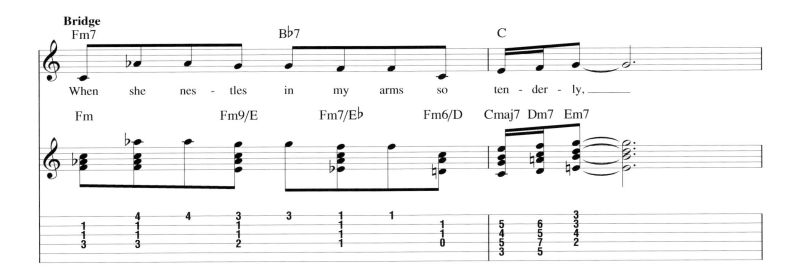

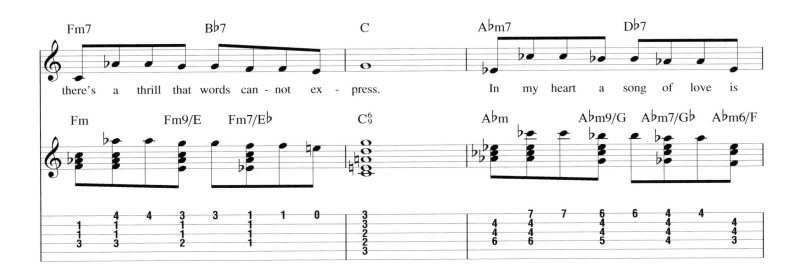

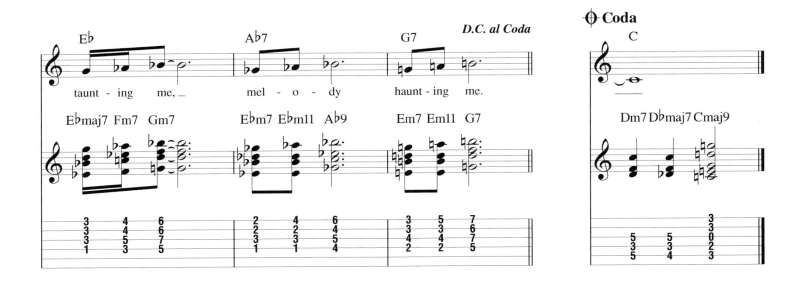

Additional Lyrics

2. Skies above me
   Never were as blue as her eyes,
   And she loves me,
   Who would want a sweeter surprise?

3. Sweet and lovely,
   Sweeter than the roses in May;
   And she loves me,
   There is nothing more I can say.

Waltz for Debby

Lyric by Gene Lees
Music by Bill Evans

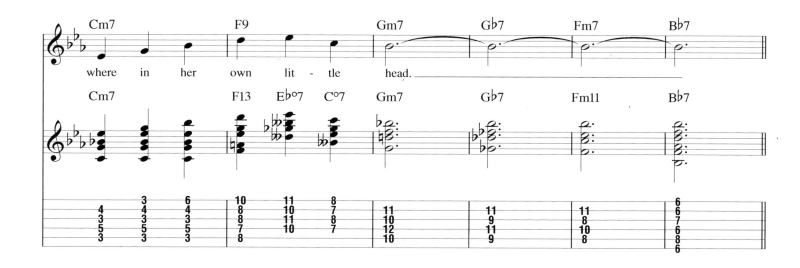

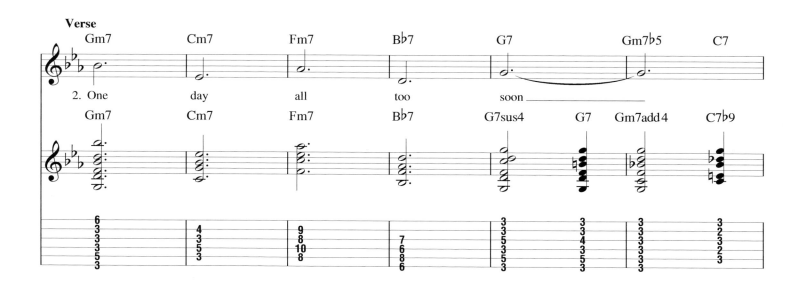

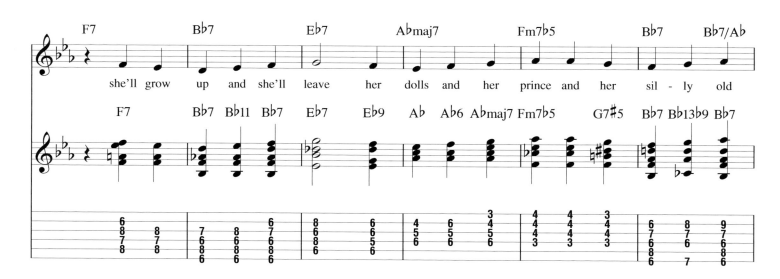

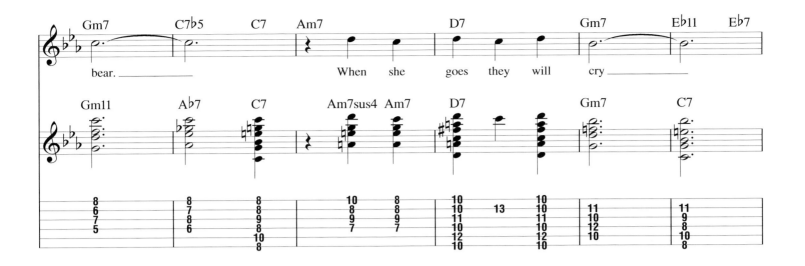

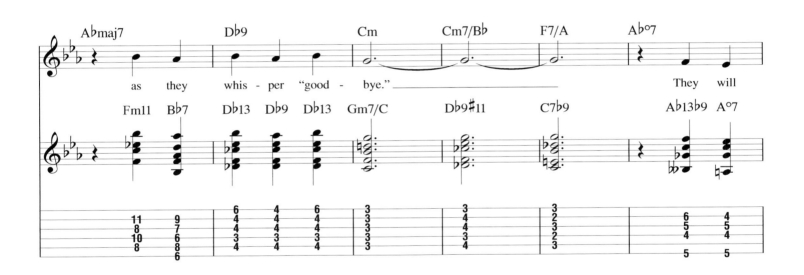

Yardbird Suite

By Charlie Parker

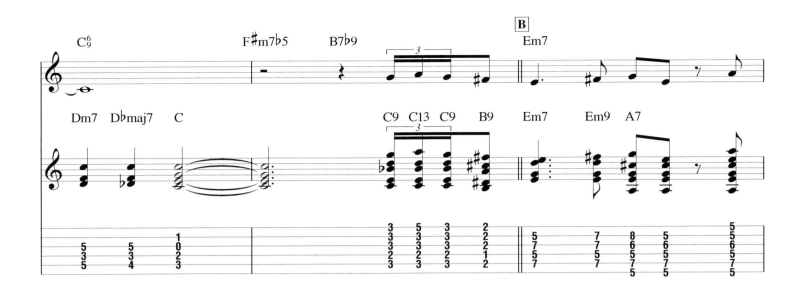

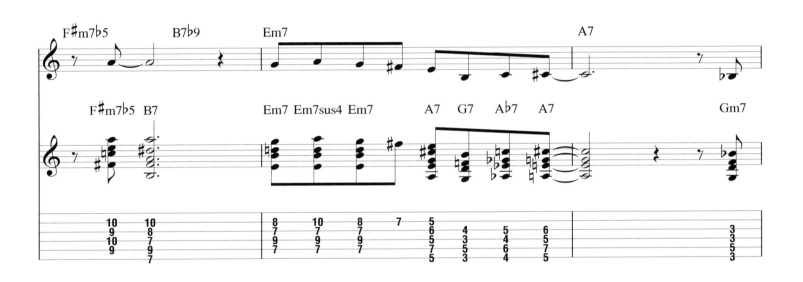

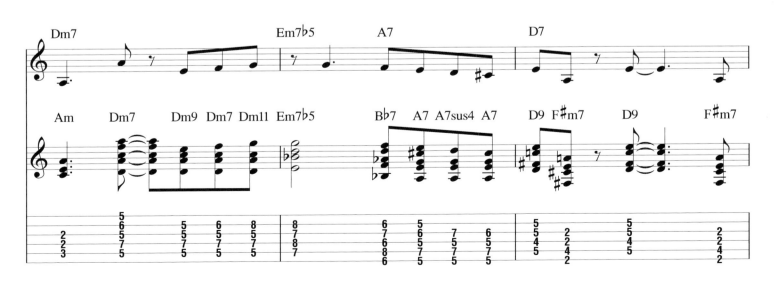

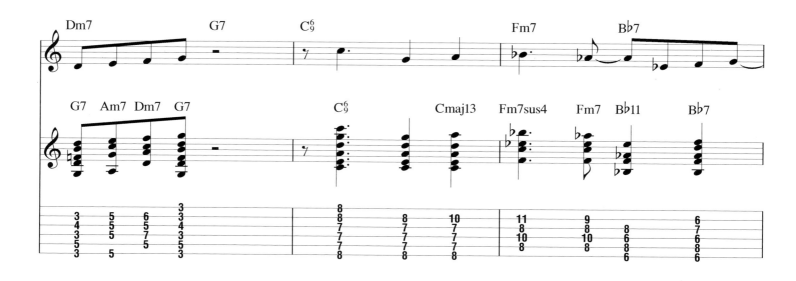

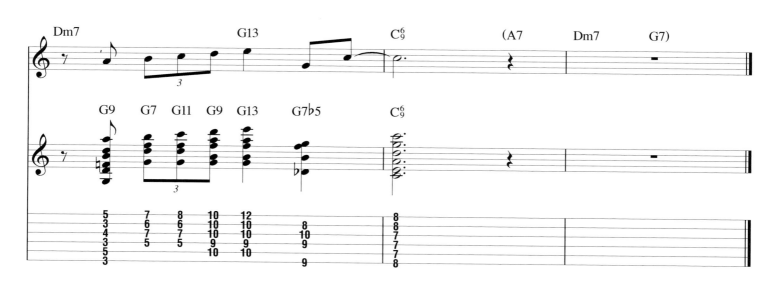

You'll Never Walk Alone

from CAROUSEL

Lyrics by Oscar Hammerstein II
Music by Richard Rodgers

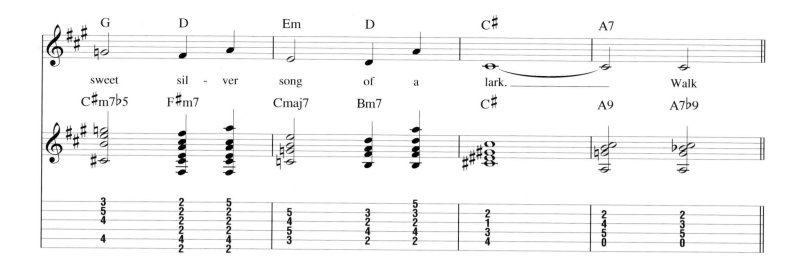

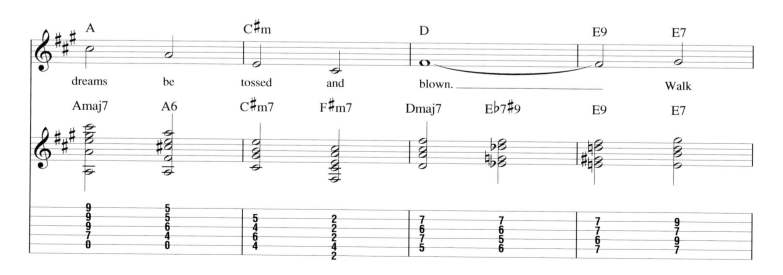

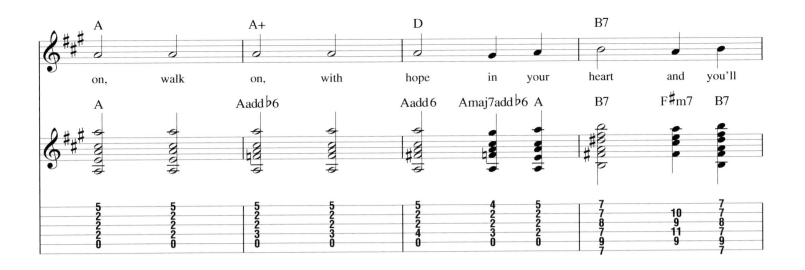

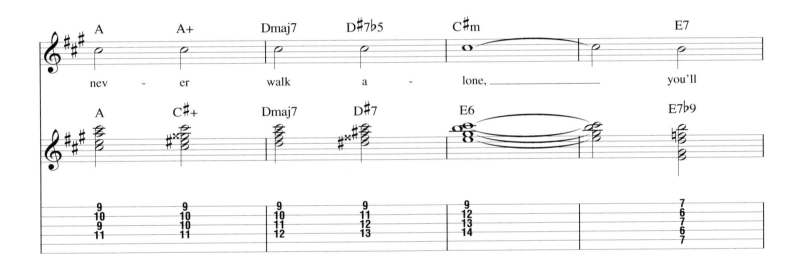

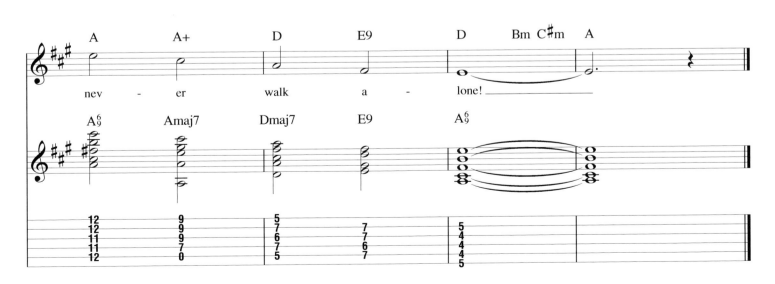

You've Changed

Words and Music by Bill Carey and Carl Fischer

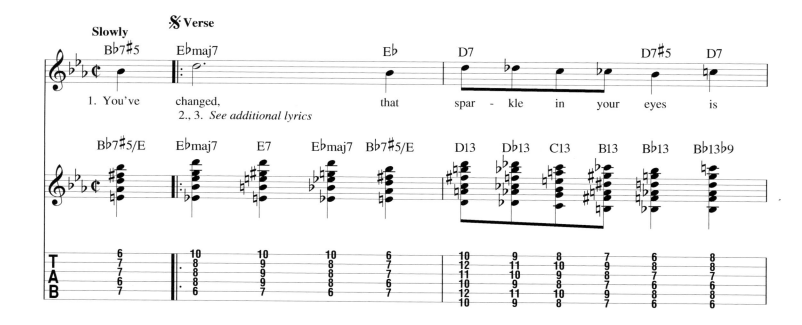

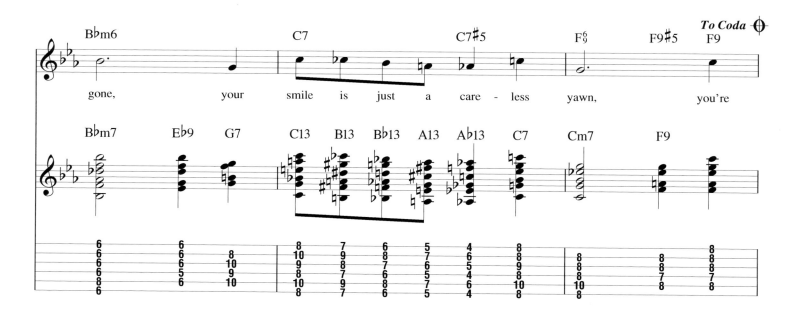

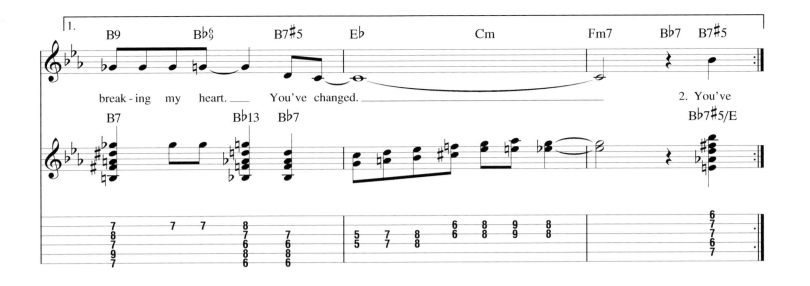

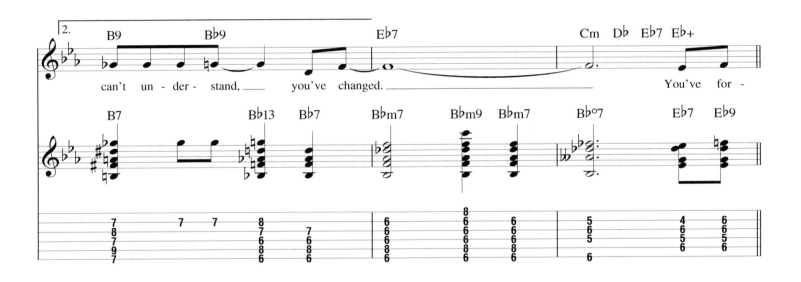

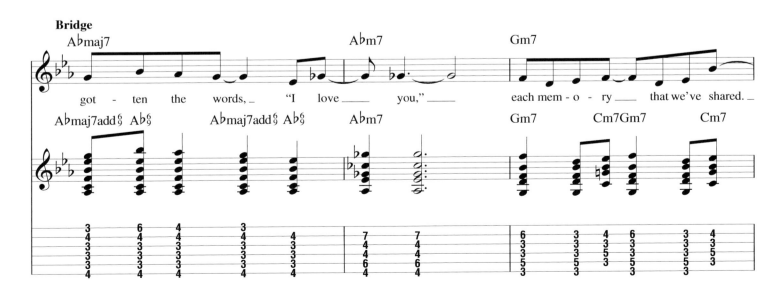

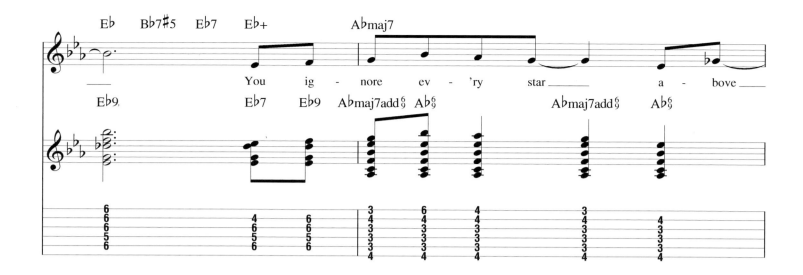

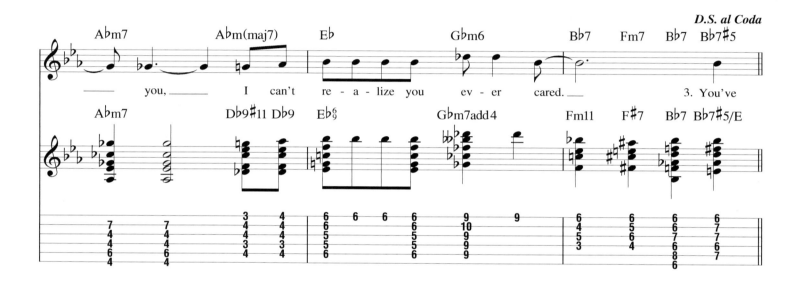

D.S. al Coda

Additional Lyrics

2. You've changed,
   Your kisses are now so blasé,
   You're bored with me in ev'ry way,
   I can't understand, you've changed.

3. You've changed,
   You're not the angel I once knew.
   No need to tell me that we're through,
   It's all over now, you've changed.

ABOUT THE AUTHOR

Robert Yelin is a guitarist, arranger, educator, and writer who has been playing jazz for over 40 years. His first inspiration came from Johnny Smith's chord-melody solos, and it was the rich variety of guitar chords that moved him to arrange nearly 2,000 songs to date. His 1982 album *Night Rain* was named best solo instrumental album in *Cadence* magazine's critics poll. *Guitar Player* wrote: "Yelin's arrangements are unique. He looks for the right chord; not the right lick. He uses alternate tunings, harmonics, and pizzicato effects tastefully while he whips through difficult passages with no sense of strain." In the liner notes for Yelin's jazz trio album *Song For My Wife*, Johnny Smith wrote: "Bob Yelin is an excellent jazz guitarist and this is an excellent album. His music leaves a lasting, musical memory."

In addition to leading the jazz guitar ensemble at the University of Colorado, Bob Yelin has had over 3,500 private students. For more than 20 years he has taught improvisation and chords through his correspondence course. He was *Guitar Player's* contributing jazz editor from 1968-1982, and his writings have also appeared in *Frets* and *Just Jazz Guitar* magazines. His bio can be found in *Who's Who in Entertainment* and the highly respected book, *The Jazz Guitar — It's Evolution, Players and Personalities Since 1900*. He has performed throughout the United States as a solo artist and with his jazz trio.

Fellow jazz great Gene Bertoncini may have put it best when he described Bob Yelin and himself as "chordiologists."

Robert Yelin plays 6, 7, and 14 string Buscarino archtop guitars.

Buscarino Guitars
2348 Wide Horizon Drive
Franklin, NC 28734
(828) 349-9867

Guitar Notation Legend

Guitar Music can be notated three different ways: on a *musical staff*, in *tablature*, and in *rhythm slashes*.

RHYTHM SLASHES are written above the staff. Strum chords in the rhythm indicated. Use the chord diagrams found at the top of the first page of the transcription for the appropriate chord voicings. Round noteheads indicate single notes.

THE MUSICAL STAFF shows pitches and rhythms and is divided by bar lines into measures. Pitches are named after the first seven letters of the alphabet.

TABLATURE graphically represents the guitar fingerboard. Each horizontal line represents a string, and each number represents a fret.

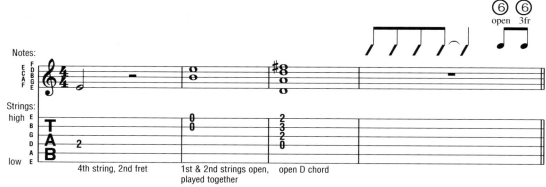

4th string, 2nd fret   1st & 2nd strings open, played together   open D chord

HALF-STEP BEND: Strike the note and bend up 1/2 step.

WHOLE-STEP BEND: Strike the note and bend up one step.

GRACE NOTE BEND: Strike the note and immediately bend up as indicated.

SLIGHT (MICROTONE) BEND: Strike the note and bend up 1/4 step.

BEND AND RELEASE: Strike the note and bend up as indicated, then release back to the original note. Only the first note is struck.

PRE-BEND: Bend the note as indicated, then strike it.

VIBRATO: The string is vibrated by rapidly bending and releasing the note with the fretting hand.

WIDE VIBRATO: The pitch is varied to a greater degree by vibrating with the fretting hand.

HAMMER-ON: Strike the first (lower) note with one finger, then sound the higher note (on the same string) with another finger by fretting it without picking.

PULL-OFF: Place both fingers on the notes to be sounded. Strike the first note and without picking, pull the finger off to sound the second (lower) note.

LEGATO SLIDE: Strike the first note and then slide the same fret-hand finger up or down to the second note. The second note is not struck.

SHIFT SLIDE: Same as legato slide, except the second note is struck.

TRILL: Very rapidly alternate between the notes indicated by continuously hammering on and pulling off.

TAPPING: Hammer ("tap") the fret indicated with the pick-hand index or middle finger and pull off to the note fretted by the fret hand.

NATURAL HARMONIC: Strike the note while the fret-hand lightly touches the string directly over the fret indicated.

PINCH HARMONIC: The note is fretted normally and a harmonic is produced by adding the edge of the thumb or the tip of the index finger of the pick hand to the normal pick attack.

PICK SCRAPE: The edge of the pick is rubbed down (or up) the string, producing a scratchy sound.

MUFFLED STRINGS: A percussive sound is produced by laying the fret hand across the string(s) without depressing, and striking them with the pick hand.

PALM MUTING: The note is partially muted by the pick hand lightly touching the string(s) just before the bridge.

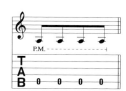

RAKE: Drag the pick across the strings indicated with a single motion.

TREMOLO PICKING: The note is picked as rapidly and continuously as possible.

VIBRATO BAR DIVE AND RETURN: The pitch of the note or chord is dropped a specified number of steps (in rhythm) then returned to the original pitch.

VIBRATO BAR SCOOP: Depress the bar just before striking the note, then quickly release the bar.

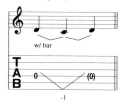

VIBRATO BAR DIP: Strike the note and then immediately drop a specified number of steps, then release back to the original pitch.

JAZZ GUITAR PUBLICATIONS
from HAL LEONARD

Berklee Jazz Standards for Solo Guitar
Berklee Press
INCLUDES TAB
Learn ten jazz guitar standards in performance-ready arrangements which demonstrate different ways to interpret jazz standards. Includes: Dedicated to You • I'm Glad There Is You • My Foolish Heart • Stella by Starlight • You Don't Know What Love Is • and more.
50449653 Book/Online Audio $22.99

Fingerpicking Early Jazz Standards
INCLUDES TAB
15 songs arranged for solo guitar in standard notation and tablature: Blue Skies • But Not for Me • Bye Bye Blackbird • I'll See You in My Dreams • Lover, Come Back to Me • Mood Indigo • Muskrat Ramble • My Melancholy Baby • On the Sunny Side of the Street • St. Louis Blues • Some of These Days • Stormy Weather (Keeps Rainin' All the Time) • Sweet Georgia Brown • When It's Sleepy Time Down South • You Took Advantage of Me.
00276565 . . . . $12.99

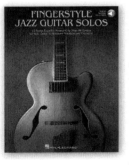

Fingerstyle Jazz Guitar Solos
INCLUDES TAB
arr. Sean McGowan
A dozen jazz classics have been expertly arranged for solo guitar in standard notation and tab: All Blues • Confirmation • Get Me to the Church on Time • I'm Old Fashioned • My Romance • On the Street Where You Live • Polka Dots and Moonbeams • Prelude to a Kiss • Ruby, My Dear • Stolen Moments • There Will Never Be Another You • Where or When.
00210455 Book/Online Audio $19.99

First 50 Jazz Standards You Should Play on Guitar
Includes: All the Things You Are • Body and Soul • Don't Get Around Much Anymore • Fly Me to the Moon (In Other Words) • The Girl from Ipanema (Garota De Ipanema) • I Got Rhythm • Laura • Misty • Night and Day • Satin Doll • Summertime • When I Fall in Love • and more.
00198594 . . . . $16.99

Jazz Classics for Easy Guitar
INCLUDES TAB
Nearly sixty jazz standards that every developing guitarist should know: As Time Goes By • But Not for Me • Fascinating Rhythm • I'm Getting Sentimental over You • In the Still of the Night • Over the Rainbow • 'S Wonderful • Someone to Watch over Me • Summertime • Taking a Chance on Love • Tea for Two • Waltz for Debby • and more.
00192503 Easy Guitar with Notes & Tab $16.99

Jazz Classics for Guitar Tab
INCLUDES TAB
51 standards for solo guitar with chord symbols: Ain't Misbehavin' • Anthropology • Birdland • Don't Get Around Much Anymore • Fascinating Rhythm • Groovin' High • How High the Moon • I Got Rhythm • Lullaby of Birdland • A Night in Tunisia • On Green Dolphin Street • Ornithology • Satin Doll • Whisper Not • and more.
00129202 . . . . $14.99

Jazz Favorites for Easy Guitar
INCLUDES TAB
60 jazz standards for beginning-level guitarists: Ain't Misbehavin' • Autumn Leaves • Body and Soul • Georgia on My Mind • How Deep Is the Ocean • Misty • My Funny Valentine • Lullaby of Birdland • Old Devil Moon • Satin Doll • Speak Low • Tenderly • The Very Thought of You • The Way You Look Tonight • Where or When • Witchcraft • and more.
00702275 Easy Guitar with Notes & Tab $17.99

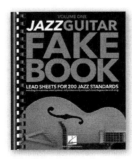

Jazz Guitar Fake Book – Volume 1
Lead sheets for 200 jazz standards: At Last • Come Sunday • Desafinado • A Fine Romance • The Girl from Ipanema (Garôta De Ipanema) • In the Mood • Lazy River • Mack the Knife • My Way • The Nearness of You • On a Slow Boat to China • Satin Doll • Stardust • Time After Time • Witchcraft • You'd Be So Nice to Come Home To • and many more.
00145418 Spiralbound. $39.99

Jazz Guitar Omnibook
INCLUDES TAB
Transcriptions for all C instruments of 30 songs: Airegin (Wes Montgomery) • Honeysuckle Rose (Django Reinhardt) • Just Friends (Pat Martino) • Night and Day (Joe Pass) • On Green Dolphin Street (Barney Kessel) • Rose Room (Charlie Christian) • What Is This Thing Called Love? (Grant Green) • Yardbird Suite (Tal Farlow) • and more.
00274203 Spiralbound $29.99

Jazz Standards for Solo Guitar
arr. Robert B. Yelin
INCLUDES TAB
35 lush chord melody arrangements in standard notation and tab: Ain't Misbehavin' • Autumn Leaves • Bewitched • Cherokee (Indian Love Song) • I've Got You Under My Skin • Lullaby of Birdland • Misty • Stella by Starlight • Tangerine • The Very Thought of You • and more.
00699277 . . . . $19.99

Smooth Jazz
Guitar Play-Along Series, Vol. 124
INCLUDES TAB
Just follow the tab, listen to the sound-alike audio, and then play along using the separate backing tracks. 8 songs: After Hours (The Antidote) (Ronny Jordan) • Breezin' (George Benson) • Cause We've Ended As Lovers (Chieli Minucci) • High Five (Chuck Loeb) • Night Rhythms (Lee Ritenour) • Smiles and Smiles to Go (Larry Carlton) • Up 'N' at 'Em (Norman Brown) • Wishful Thinking (Earl Klugh).
00200664 Book/Online Audio $17.99

Solo Jazz Guitar Standards
arr. Matt Otten
INCLUDES TAB
16 jazz guitar selections in standard notation and tab: Beautiful Love • Comecar De Novo • Days of Wine and Roses • Dolphin Dance • Estate • How Insensitive (Insensatez) • In Love in Vain • Laurie • Lover Man (Oh, Where Can You Be?) • My Foolish Heart • My Funny Valentine • My One and Only Love • My Romance • Nature Boy • Never Let Me Go • You Must Believe in Spring.
00198371 Book/Online Audio $22.99

HAL•LEONARD®
Order today at **halleonard.com**

IMPROVE YOUR IMPROV

AND OTHER JAZZ TECHNIQUES WITH BOOKS FROM HAL LEONARD

JAZZ GUITAR
HAL LEONARD GUITAR METHOD
by Jeff Schroedl

The Hal Leonard Jazz Guitar Method is your complete guide to learning jazz guitar. This book uses real jazz songs to teach the basics of accompanying and improvising jazz guitar in the style of Wes Montgomery, Joe Pass, Tal Farlow, Charlie Christian, Pat Martino, Barney Kessel, Jim Hall, and many others.
00695359 Book/Online Audio $22.99

AMAZING PHRASING
50 WAYS TO IMPROVE YOUR
IMPROVISATIONAL SKILLS • *by Tom Kolb*

This book explores all the main components necessary for crafting well-balanced rhythmic and melodic phrases. It also explains how these phrases are put together to form cohesive solos. Many styles are covered – rock, blues, jazz, fusion, country, Latin, funk and more – and all of the concepts are backed up with musical examples.
00695583 Book/Online Audio $22.99

BEST OF JAZZ GUITAR
by Wolf Marshall • Signature Licks

In this book/audio pack, Wolf Marshall provides a hands-on analysis of 10 of the most frequently played tunes in the jazz genre, as played by the leading guitarists of all time. Each selection includes technical analysis and performance notes, biographical sketches, and authentic matching audio with backing tracks.
00695586 Book/Online Audio $29.99

CHORD-MELODY PHRASES FOR GUITAR
by Ron Eschete • REH ProLessons Series

Expand your chord-melody chops with these outstanding jazz phrases! This book covers: chord substitutions, chromatic movements, contrary motion, pedal tones, inner-voice movements, reharmonization techniques, and much more. Includes standard notation and tab, and online audio.
00695628 Book/Online Audio $17.99

CHORDS FOR JAZZ GUITAR
THE COMPLETE GUIDE TO COMPING,
CHORD MELODY AND CHORD SOLOING • *by Charlton Johnson*

This book/audio pack will teach you how to play jazz chords all over the fretboard in a variety of styles and progressions. It covers: voicings, progressions, jazz chord theory, comping, chord melody, chord soloing, voice leading and many more topics. The audio offers 98 full-band demo tracks. No tablature.
00695706 Book/Online Audio $19.99

FRETBOARD ROADMAPS – JAZZ GUITAR
THE ESSENTIAL GUITAR PATTERNS
THAT ALL THE PROS KNOW AND USE • *by Fred Sokolow*

This book will get guitarists playing lead & rhythm anywhere on the fretboard, in any key! It teaches a variety of lead guitar styles using moveable patterns, double-note licks, sliding pentatonics and more, through easy-to-follow diagrams and instructions. The online audio includes 54 full-demo tracks.
00695354 Book/Online Audio $17.99

JAZZ IMPROVISATION FOR GUITAR
by Les Wise • REH ProLessons Series

This book/audio will allow you to make the transition from playing disjointed scales and arpeggios to playing melodic jazz solos that maintain continuity and interest for the listener. Topics covered include: tension and resolution, major scale, melodic minor scale, and harmonic minor scale patterns, common licks and substitution techniques, creating altered tension, and more! Features standard notation and tab, and online audio.
00695657 Book/Online Audio $19.99

JAZZ RHYTHM GUITAR
THE COMPLETE GUIDE
by Jack Grassel

This book/audio pack will help rhythm guitarists better understand: chord symbols and voicings, comping styles and patterns, equipment, accessories and set-up, the fingerboard, chord theory, and much more. The accompanying online audio includes 74 full-band tracks.
00695654 Book/Online Audio $24.99

JAZZ SOLOS FOR GUITAR
LEAD GUITAR IN THE STYLES OF TAL FARLOW,
BARNEY KESSEL, WES MONTGOMERY, JOE PASS, JOHNNY SMITH
by Les Wise

Examine the solo concepts of the masters with this book including phrase-by-phrase performance notes, tips on arpeggio substitution, scale substitution, tension and resolution, jazz-blues, chord soloing, and more. The audio includes full demonstration and rhythm-only tracks.
00695447 Book/Online Audio $19.99

100 JAZZ LESSONS
Guitar Lesson Goldmine Series
by John Heussenstamm and Paul Silbergleit

Featuring 100 individual modules covering a giant array of topics, each lesson includes detailed instruction with playing examples presented in standard notation and tablature. You'll also get extremely useful tips, scale diagrams, and more to reinforce your learning experience, plus audio featuring performance demos of all the examples in the book!
00696454 Book/Online Audio $24.99

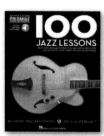

101 MUST-KNOW JAZZ LICKS
A QUICK, EASY REFERENCE GUIDE
FOR ALL GUITARISTS • *by Wolf Marshall*

Here are 101 definitive licks, plus demonstration audio, from every major jazz guitar style, neatly organized into easy-to-use categories. They're all here: swing and pre-bop, bebop, post-bop modern jazz, hard bop and cool jazz, modal jazz, soul jazz and postmodern jazz. Includes an introduction, tips, and a list of suggested recordings.
00695433 Book/Online Audio $19.99

SWING AND BIG BAND GUITAR
FOUR-TO-THE-BAR COMPING IN THE STYLE OF
FREDDIE GREEN • *by Charlton Johnson*

This unique package teaches the essentials of swing and big band styles, including chord voicings, inversions, substitutions; time and groove, reading charts, chord reduction, and expansion; sample songs, patterns, progressions, and exercises; chord reference library; and online audio with over 50 full-demo examples. Uses chord grids – no tablature.
00695147 Book/Online Audio $22.99

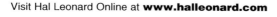

Visit Hal Leonard Online at **www.halleonard.com**

*Prices, contents and availability
subject to change without notice.*